YOUR CALIFORNIA GARDEN

AND MINE

Your California Garden

AND MINE

by

SYDNEY B. MITCHELL

M. BARROWS AND COMPANY, INC.

New York

To
Quincy R. Westfall
my gardener
without whose help and interest
I could hardly have a garden
in these later years

CONTENTS

Contents

Contents

Contents

LIST OF ILLUSTRATIONS

FOREWORD

This is a new book, not a revision of my earlier ones, *Gardening in California* and *From a Sunset Garden*, now both out of print. It is not a manual, and it doesn't tell everything about gardening in California—that would take a dozen books or more—but it has been written for California amateurs with their interests and their conditions in mind. I have tried to combine in it much of what made one of these earlier books appeal to the beginner, along with the more advanced material of the other, but it contains also many years of later experience in California gardening. Parts of a few chapters have appeared in the *Journal of the California Horticultural Society*, and I would normally have to thank the editor for permission to use them, were he and I not the same person. I do wish, however, to acknowledge a debt—in some cases mentioned specifically in the book—to the fine definitive treatments of the culture of certain plants which appeared there, and to thank many gardening friends for their contributions to my horticultural education.

For the patient labor of getting the manuscript into a state acceptable to the publisher, I have, as always, to thank my wife.

SYDNEY B. MITCHELL

Berkeley, 1947

YOUR CALIFORNIA GARDEN

AND MINE

CHAPTER ONE

GARDENING, PARTICULARLY IN CALIFORNIA

———

ARDENING is a very personal affair, and your garden and mine, if they are really our own, are likely to be extensions of our personalities, opportunities for self-expression, wonderful at best, harmless at least, where there will be by-products of beauty and of utility and of healthful recreation. It follows that this will be a pretty personal book for both of us. You will want to get from it what will interest and help you, and I will put into it, in the main, my own experience of gardening, chiefly in California. It is limited to ornamental gardening, and the emphasis is on the variety of plants we have available for our gardens and their particular needs here. I have always gardened for fun, and growing vegetables I have left to those who enjoy it. You have the right to be the kind of gardener you are—even to abstain totally from gardening if you prefer other things. If you are conservative, you may limit your interest to grass and evergreen shrubs and materials which can be depended on for the same effect, the one you like, throughout the whole year. If you are meticulous, your garden will have a perfection mine has always lacked. Your lawn will always be weedless and to keep it so will be your aim, while I consider lawns, especially in California, a compromise, sometimes a necessary evil, the care and cutting of which I hope

3

always to be able to delegate to somebody else. You may be adventurous, interested in new plans or plants, collecting and discarding, experimenting always—then your garden will show this, as mine does.

CONSIDER THE CLIMATE

It is desirable, however, that a gardener, unless his idea of fun is a lifetime fight with nature, give careful consideration, in planning his garden and choosing his interests in it, to his climate over which he admittedly has no control, to the contours of his garden which can only be altered, if at all, at great and generally unwarranted cost, and to his soils which can be cultivated and improved in texture and fertility, but which may have inherent limitations that he may as well recognize.

In California, particularly if he is a recent arrival here, he will have to learn to accept our climate, a Mediterranean type, of two seasons, a warm dry summer and a cool wet winter, and work with rather than against it. Moreover, inasmuch as California climates vary to a degree hardly understandable to people brought up east of the Sierras, a gardener here must study his own conditions, annual rainfall, maximum heat and cold, sunshine and fog, all greatly affecting what he can grow and how successfully. For instance, fuchsias belong to the cool coastal belt, oleanders to the warm interior. He will above all have to face the fact that, however unusual the weather may be, we can always count on a long summer drought, five rainless months or more, and this means constant watering to keep most gardens going through it. Even our lack of winter cold he will find not wholly an asset, as most deciduous shrubs and many perennials prefer the enforced rest that winter gives

4

them. However, our climate has many compensations besides the ease of living in it. One of these is the lack of severe winter cold and the consequent ability to grow outdoors a wider range of plants than in gardens elsewhere. This is in fact almost a liability as we have really an embarrassment of materials with which to concern ourselves or paint our garden pictures. To me our greatest climatic advantage is the long cool period, particularly on the coast, where spring extends from Thanksgiving to Decoration Day, and the pace of development is so slow that we can have daffodils for three months and bearded iris for two, rather than the rush of the eastern American spring hurrying into summer. The cool summers also found in certain sections, around San Francisco Bay and along the coast all the way south, continue this pleasant leisurely procession of summer flowers in a way not possible where, at that time of year, the gardener has to take heat waves and heavy rains with their devastating aftermaths.

SIZE, CONTOUR, SOIL

The size and the contours of his garden will also considerably affect not only planning but planting. A small level garden may have certain limitations, but it is easier to plan, especially as an open center with trees and shrubs mainly around the edges for framing and shutting the place in; it is also easier to get around in and to maintain throughout the year. A steep garden may be more exciting or inspiring, but it involves terraces or the shrub planting of slopes—grass being difficult here on edge—and it is harder to care for, particularly if it faces west and so gets baked in summer.

If soils are heavy and intractable, it may be possible to improve them by the incorporation of humus and sand, but if the place is large this is too big a job, and most of it had better be planted to such shrubs, perennials, and bulbs as accept the natural soil, with only smaller areas specially prepared for those demanding lighter soil. Where soil is very sandy, it must get humus and fertilizer, but it will be easy to work, and many annuals and certain bulbs and tubers, dahlias for example, will be pleased with it.

TYPE OF PLANTING

A gardener should also, when planning his garden—even earlier in choosing the area of his activities—give thought to what he primarily wants. This may be just an extension to the house, an outdoor living area; it may be a frame for the house, an orderly uncluttered place; or it may be, in the main, a cutting garden, which will greatly affect the choice of things to be grown; or again it may be for the intensive cultivation of some specialty—azaleas, dahlias, irises, roses, succulents. Of course some of these may be combined; but in planning even a small garden, these purposes may readily be separated, and the cut flowers or the specialties put in the rear or farthest away from the house.

Do not try to have your garden a blaze of color twelve months of the year; if your garden does not need a rest, you do. If your garden is on a steep slope or if you want to be fairly free in summer to spend week ends away from it or take long vacations, emphasize winter and spring, which, horticultur- ally speaking, is the cream of the year in California, and carry through the summer without too constant need of watering, weeding, and other care. In any case, unless you have an aw- ful lot of energy to work off, emphasize ease, don't let the garden be your master. This will mean the planting of trees

6

and a large use of evergreen shrubs, of bulbs—particularly those of spring flowering—and of herbaceous perennials, and a limited growing of annuals and of other things which require regular lifting, division, and replanting. Rock gardens and pots are for puttering, a pleasant and legitimate use of time, if you have lots of it. Above all, work with nature, and grow in general those things which interest you and do well under your conditions.

GARDEN FACILITIES

In your garden, think of conveniences, as planners do of kitchens. It should be of easy access, so that you can get into it quickly from the house and get around it with the greatest of ease. Facility of watering is of great help. Permanent sprinkler installations for lawns and for fuchsia and azalea beds—even for cutting gardens of gladiolus or such summer flowers—many hose bibs, and short hoses for other parts of the garden will all help to cut down work; also, easy waste disposals, areas at the back or side for composting weeds and herbaceous trimmings, and, if the garden is small, a ready way to get woody prunings carried off, or perhaps an incinerator. Tools should be kept where they are reasonably central to the place of their use. An outdoor tool house, combined with frames, a small lath house, and even what the English call a bit of glass might be made into a unit as convenient as those refrigerator, stove, and sink units for kitchens. We need the attention of planners for the convenience of doing our own work, now that labor is hard to pay for in the garden as well as in the house.

Science in the garden is coming to the aid of the gardener. Better tools, better sprays, better insecticides, more specialized chemical fertilizers, and weed killers are on the way, and no future Kipling will need to sing of those who dig weeds out of paths with kitchen knives; they will just spray or water them out. Even if a good gardener does spend a great deal of time on his knees, it is not a penance but a pleasant pursuit, and advantage should be taken of modern methods, now that there are enough gardeners to justify special efforts to ease their labors.

FASHIONS IN GARDENING

There are fashions in flowers and styles in gardening, just as there are fashions in clothes and styles in domestic architecture. Even a male gardener can rejoice that he grew up in and out of the period of Brussels carpets in houses and carpet bedding in gardens—they came together—and that he lives in a time when excessive and meaningless decoration of homes, outside and in, has given place to simplicity and purity. Now the pendulum has swung so far that it is possible to have gardens of a kind which are nearly as complete, as finished, and as permanent when the landscape architect turns them over to their owners, as are some of the very modern houses. But to me gardening as an avocation, a recreation, is so concerned with life and color, with the change in seasons and in my interests, that it involves a certain complexity and a variety of materials and will never be really finished—until I am.

MY GARDEN IN BERKELEY

Because this book is based so largely on the nearly twenty-five years of experience in our present garden, it is well that those who read it should know something of the conditions under which we work and what we have done here. But this experience was preceded by years of gardening in Montreal, in commercial horticulture near Boston, and in earlier, smaller, and very different California gardens—one on the level adobe soil of the campus of Stanford University, the other on the thin soil of a westward facing slope looking to the Golden Gate from the lower Berkeley hills.

Our present garden is nearly a thousand feet up in the Berkeley hills, just over the top in Contra Costa County, about three miles north of the University of California campus. It faces east and slopes down to Wildcat Canyon, now become the Tilden Regional Park. Our climate is cool and stimulating, with only a few degrees of frost in winter and almost no hot summer weather. The annual rainfall averages about twenty-four inches, but it has been as high as thirty-nine inches and as low as twelve in "unusual" years. We get more sunshine in the morning than we do in late afternoon because the top of the hill is right above us to the west. For the same reason, we get much less wind from the Pacific than does Berkeley, perhaps more high fog in the summer evenings, and none of the low or tule fog of winter days. The garden is almost square, about two hundred feet along the road and the same depth, but we own the acre below us, which is mostly still uncultivated and considerably covered with eucalyptus, which gives a backdrop and skyline. The soil, a couple of feet deep, overlying clay, is a rather heavy black loam, fairly rich, neutral, and easy to cultivate: it is also very slippery when wet. When we built here, only one other house was visible, on the hilltop to the north of us, and even now it is a rather rural area, as the Salbach Gardens adjoin us on the south, and the canyon and the mountains which form our view are a part

9

of the aforementioned regional park and are kept in a natural state.

There is a rather sharp drop just below the road, so we built our original garage to the north, on the road level, with rough stone steps and a double steppingstone path down to the house, which is of white stucco and somewhat suggests a small Spanish farmhouse with red tile roof, nearly window-less front, and a patio formed by the bedroom wing. This patio is now paved with brick, a more satisfactory surface than the former grass, and far easier to maintain. It is framed on the two open sides by a low hedge of the evergreen Lonicera nitida. The house occupies the most nearly level place we could find or make, close to and just below the road. The garage is now a guest cottage, and our automobile is housed in a purely functional shelter to the south of the house and on the same level, as climbing up to the original one proved too tough for us. The new garage is already somewhat screened by fuchsias and camellias, and has a Mermaid rose and a white wisteria growing on it.

To create a quite level space in front of the house, we had to dig back a bit into the hill, which is now supported by a stone wall against which azaleas are very happy. The flat area between it and the house is divided into a small strip of grass, Colonial bent, nearest the wall, and a flagged terrace— not of stone but of concrete slabs in a good design—laid out and poured where they lie. The grass extends into the inter-stices between these artificial stones and does require occasional cutting, but we find it can be done by machine. My one-time Italian gardener could never see why I didn't fill them in with concrete and make one solid slab, and I never felt it worth while trying to explain to him that I was aiming to make a gradual transition from house to lawn. We have also two small pieces of grass to the south of the house on different levels, to provide open areas, and these are nearly bordered by azaleas and other moisture-loving plants. The steep bank in front of the house, running up to the road, is planted with shrubs requiring no care and no water—Japanese quinces, rock roses, and brooms in variety, abelias, barberries, and cotoneasters. It gives a pleasant evergreen foliage effect from the house and completely shuts out the road above; in fact, it is one of the most successful functional plantings I have ever seen.

BACKGROUNDS

When we began our garden, there were a few eucalyptus scattered thinly over the area. We removed most of those not on the boundaries and eventually all of them. Much foolishness has been written about the toxic character of eucalyptus. In general they are undesirable only because they reach out in summer for all the adjacent moisture and because they are very untidy trees, always shedding bark and leaves and small branches, even large ones during winter winds and rain. The cost of continually cleaning up after them was unjustified. But, as a matter of experiment, I planted daffodils right under them, and they did well because in winter there was moisture enough for all and in summer the daffodils were dormant. Young Monterey pines we found could even compete with them in summer, and these eventually replaced them for boundary plantings on both upper ends of the property. The Montereys were the most satisfactory of our native pines, quick growing and dark green in color. Along the northwest margin

we tried other natives, but found the Monterey cypress un-
certain and lost several, due to an incurable disease. Toyons,
too, were given up because they became disfigured. At the
bottom of the property on the north side, from which we get
our cold winter and dry summer winds, we planted groups of
redwoods, madrona, and the common evergreen oak, Quercus
agrifolia. All have made wonderful growth in twenty years
from the little pot plants we started with, and visitors imagine
that the large spreading oaks must be at least a hundred years
old. All these natives grow quickly if cared for, and no one
starting a garden in middle life should hesitate to plant them,
common opinion to the contrary.

A HOME ORCHARD

On the south side is a small home orchard, now nearly limited to apples, as peaches, apricots, and pears were not very
good because our summers were too cool. Underneath them
we plant hyacinths, scillas, and daffodils in large casual groups,
which give a pleasant natural effect in spring when the fruit
trees are leafless. The planting around the house and on the
patio is mainly of evergreen shrubs. Azaleas and camellias
predominate, with a good many fuchsias interplanted for summer color. In the upper part of the garden there are a great
many flowering fruit trees and magnolias which are the glory
of the place in their seasons. The garden below the house is
a series of horizontal bands. We found that in a hillside garden
it was easier to get around by having paths across it on the
level, curving down from one to another, than to have deep
vertical paths or expensive steps and terraces. Because of the
slope, we have used mostly in the paths the round flat step-
pingstones of the type sometimes called "bride's biscuits";

these are poured where they are to stand and, unlike gravel, do not wash away. The horizontal plantings are now mainly given up to daffodils for February and March, and irises for April and May, and are separated and backed by shrubbery plantings which need little or no care. The general idea is that the garden blooms on its outskirts in winter and early spring, and in the middle areas later; by summer these levels can be forgotten, and summer effort, watering, and care limited to the area around the house. This arrangement keeps down expense of watering and weeding, and favors large remote spaces for the spring flowers, which are now the main interest of the owners.

In the chapters which follow, I have endeavored to pass on something of what I have learned in nearly forty years of varied California gardening, and to interpret my experience in such a way that it may be of value to gardeners anywhere in our state. The possibilities under our conditions are so great that no one book can honestly claim to include everything, indeed no honest gardener can say he knows it all. One of the greatest advantages of gardening is the fact that it is a life-time pursuit in which you are always a participant. You are never forced into the grandstand as physical vigor declines; your interest and knowledge increase with the years.

CHAPTER TWO

FLOWERING FRUIT TREES AND MAGNOLIAS

O EMPHASIZE the change of seasons and take every advantage of our long cool central California spring, we have planted a variety of deciduous flowering fruit trees with spring-flowering bulbs under them. Visitors to Berkeley in February or March are thrilled with the lovely color along certain streets which were planted with flowering plums, peaches, or cherries a few years ago by the city. They flower when quite young, the plums and peaches almost at once; they extend in their blooming time over a period of three months if the proper selection of varieties is made, and in turn each gives lovely garden color that is relatively little affected by the rains which muddy flowers on the ground. Because they lose their leaves in winter—many of them flower on the bare branches—these trees let in the sun all winter, so they can be planted right up against the south side of the house. In private gardens, the ground beneath them is available for spring-flowering bulbs. The combination of ground color with that above in the trees is the feature of our garden in spring. This is one of the easiest of all forms of flower gardening; once established, its maintenance is far less than where herbaceous plants are used.

I have elected to treat flowering fruit trees in groups beginning with the earliest, but it should be realized that the late ones of one group overlap the earliest ones of another, and that some crab-apples and cherries are in flower at the same time.

APRICOTS, PEACHES, ALMONDS

Our first flowering fruit trees are apricots. In late January, a double deep-glowing pink begins to bloom along all the upright and bare brown branches. This is the form of Prunus armeniaca distributed under the name Charles Abraham, its introducer to our gardens. We have it grafted on an unfruitful peach and an indifferent fruiting plum, and it has done wonderfully on both. Before it is over, the beautiful, double white Japanese apricot Rosemary Clarke, a member of the P. Mume group, begins and is at its best in early February. The third and last apricot we grow is the double pink Dawn, a most beautiful and effective little tree of the Mume section. These apricots are far too seldom grown, for they introduce spring to our gardens.

Still, in many gardens the first flowering fruit trees are the plums. Prunus Pissardi, tall, slender, purple-leaved, with small single near-white flowers, we do not grow, because we don't want too many purple-leaved trees, and this one seems particularly dull and dusty in summer. We prefer Prunus Blireana, a smaller, broader purple-leaved plum; its double pink flowers appear almost as early and are much longer lasting. It and the somewhat similar P. Moseri are very effectively used in street plantings on upper Euclid Avenue in Berkeley.

We have not planted flowering peaches as freely as we might have done, perhaps because peaches have never done as well in this garden as have other fruit trees. The necessity, too, of spraying them every winter before flowering to combat the leaf curl somewhat deterred us. Lately we have experimented with some double red and double white seedlings given us and found that very heavy pruning after flowering—or what is the same thing, cutting branches for house decoration—results in a new growth almost free of peach curl. But we are not as fond of peaches in our garden as of some other things; they tend to assert themselves rather than blend into the garden picture. However, in many parts of California, particularly where summers are warmer than with us, they would be first choice of the flowering fruit trees, for they do have great advantages in that they alone are really satisfactory when branches are cut for decoration and also that by themselves they will give a long season of bloom if the proper sequence of varieties is grown. First early is San Jose Pink, then the Early Double Red, doubtless the most grown of all, and the very lovely soft pink Aurora; for later bloom, grow the Double Red, Double White, Burbank or Clara Meyer, rather similar pinks, or if you can get it, Helen Borchers, easily the finest double pink I have ever seen and a vigorous grower and free bloomer.

Flowering with the early red peach is a double pale pink almond. This almond gets no leaf curl, so needs no spraying, and it is a much stronger grower than any peach. Planted to shade our patio, its tall, wide umbrella head now covers a large area of the roof and makes a lovely cloud of pale pink, visible even from the road. Its bare branches shut out no winter sun, but when in leaf it shades our living room, screens the patio, and keeps off westerly winds.

CRAB-APPLES

I believe we have grown most of the flowering crab-apples available. They are admittedly less spectacular than peaches or cherries as the leaves come out with the flowers and the latter are generally single, yet some of them are among our most cherished trees, for not only are they graceful and lovely in flower but when in full fruit in late summer and early autumn, they give us much red and gold color, warm in distinction to the coolness of their spring bloom. Moreover the little apples make excellent jelly, just as good as do the Siberian crabs we grow especially for their fruit, and they ripen gradually and later.

The first to flower here is Pyrus floribunda, a somewhat bushy small tree which can be trained to a good branched head. Its buds are deep pink, but the flowers open out much paler and finish white; its yellow fruits are small, like marbles, late, and beloved of the quail when they get old and soft —the fruits, not the quail. We prefer this of the earlier crab-apples, but there are several quite similar ones. Pyrus Halliana, its variety P. Parkmannii, and its reputed hybrid, P. atrosanguinea, we grow but do not consider essential. The latter as it develops here is a droopy tree with deep pink flowers, but it is certainly not dark or bloody as its varietal name might imply. We grow also Pyrus Scheideckeri, possibly a double form of P. floribunda, but a smaller tree here, slow growing and much later. We do not think it essential; perhaps we are prejudiced because it was planted where its yearly crop of innumerable little apples drops along a path, underfoot and messy. It is desirable to avoid this annoyance in placing your trees.

We have also an early crab-apple with the deepest purple foliage and darkest flowers and fruit in our garden, a strong upright grower. It is probably what Bailey lists as P. purpurea, accounted a hybrid between P. sylvestris var. Niedzwetskyana and P. atrosanguinea. The parent with the, to us, unpronounceable name is the large, dark red rose-fleshed apple from Turkestan, which is one of the parents of the two rather similar crab-apples, Pyrus Eleyi and P. aldenhamensis. They are among the last to flower here and are alike in being good small trees with lively red foliage, tending to a bronzy green as the season advances, large rose-red flowers and large deep cherry red fruits in profusion. In previous gardens, we grew the double form of the American Pyrus ionesis called Bechtel's crab. Its large double pink flowers appear late among the leaves of the rather dwarf tree and suggest roses. It is lovely for a short time, but as the flowers fade to a rusty brown and hang on for a while, it didn't seem to justify a place in this garden. If we could have only two crab-apples, my choice would be Pyrus floribunda (early) and P. Eleyi (late). Fortunately we still have room here for others, and I am now trying out a set of hybrids (between P. baccata, the Siberian crab grown for its fruit, and P. Niedzwetskyana) from the Dominion Experimental Station at Morden, Manitoba, where we saw them and were excited by their large flowers and fine clear pinks and reds in a wide range of shades previously unknown to us. We have found flowering crab-apples healthy, easy to grow, and needing only enough pruning to keep the trees shapely. They possess garden value for both the spring color of flowers and the autumn color of fruit, not to mention the household value of the latter.

FLOWERING CHERRIES

Of the flowering fruit trees, doubtless the aristocrats are the cherries. Here I have found the Japanese cherries do very well, though, as seems to be their nature, some varieties are far better growers than others. Prunus campanulata, the Formosa cherry, is the first to flower here, its rosy red bell-shaped flowers, nearly the color of some of the early red peaches, coming just before or with the leaves in February. Apparently it does well in southern California where the real Japanese cherries are less happy. Continuing with the single forms of Prunus subhirtella, I do not have the fall-flowering one but a bushlike small tree with pale single flowers, pleasant but not at all exciting. The single weeping cherries are also, I believe, forms of P. subhirtella. I grew and lost other weeping cherries, but I am happy in still having Beni-shidare which arches up from the top graft before drooping, so that its trailing branches barely reach the ground. I would buy weeping cherries on as tall standard stems as I could, and if I had a pool, I would plant them on its margin, where they seem to fit better than in the open garden. I understand that with the proper stock, whatever that may be, they are long-lived and grow into large trees.

If I could have only one flowering cherry it would be the single Prunus yedoensis (syn. Yoshino), the one most largely planted along the Potomac in Washington. Ours is a pale almost white form, but the rosy inside base of the petals suggests pink. Though moved here when its trunk was at least six inches through and then heavily pruned, it established beautifully and in due time, after it had made a new top, it settled down to its dependable annual flowering, the glory of the garden. It is a tall shapely tree—as many Japanese cherries are not—and when, leafless, it flowers, it seems draped in pale pink lace. In the fall, it is equally attractive because then its leaves color beautifully. It is a rapid grower. This form of P. yedoensis is early, but from W. B. Clarke I got a later form called Akebono (Daybreak), pink, not white, and with larger flowers. I am glad our place is big enough for us to have both, for I know no better garden investment than this cherry.

Quite different from either of these, a strong vigorous tree, with long erect branches and growth suggesting the fruit cherry of commerce is a really fine large-flowered deeper pink single which I bought, nameless, in 1912. Walter Clarke took scions of it a few years ago and introduced it as Mitchell's Single Pink, for lack of its real name, but I later identified it as Mikuruma-Gaeshi, and it is now so listed. In late March or early April the three trees I have of it are a glorious sight.

The double-flowering Japanese cherries are as a whole less shapely and vigorous trees. Some have rather broad heads, wide in proportion to their height; others have a somewhat ungainly habit of stretching out long branches. But their flowers are so different from anything else in our gardens, so rich and exotic, that a few of the best are certainly worth growing. From those I have tried and of which I have the names—several others came in the way of nameless grafts from friends' gardens—I would select four pink doubles for their evident differences and the long season they cover among them, and one white double.

Tanko-shinju (Pink Pearl) is our earliest double, a good grower, one of the most shapely trees among the doubles, a regular and profuse bloomer with large soft pink fluffy flowers. Next in this locality comes Shirofugen (Victory), with pink flowers, fading white but finishing deeper pink, a good grower and bloomer. Shogetsu (Pine Moon) is my favorite among the doubles, paler than others, very free flowering in large clusters which hang below the leaves; the growth is only moderate. As the tree is rather low and broad, and one would like to look up into it, we have grafted it recently on some very tall standards. Kanzan (syn. Sekiyama and Hizakura) is a deep pink, very round and double and late, but though it seems to be more grown than most Japanese cherries, I like it less than some of the earlier and more informal doubles. The one double white we grow is Shirotae (Mt. Fuji), a vigorous but rather gawky grower with the habit of giving single flowers until it is mature, but after that a regular and wonderful double cherry to bloom. Since it branches low, we put ours on the upper rather than the lower side of the path so that we can look up at the dripping clusters of flowers as they turn pure white.

Japanese cherries are almost always grafted or budded on a more vigorous stock, and there is much discussion as to which is best. I have P. yedoensis on its own roots, grafted on Mazzard, and even grafted on a Bing fruiting cherry, and all these trees are doing well, but yedoensis is more adaptable than most cherries. We have grown the single Mikuruma-Gaeshi grafted on Mazzard stock—and it has done amazingly well, probably because it is naturally very vigorous; but where an unidentified double was put on Mazzard, the stock has grown so much thicker than the wood of the graft that the trees look as if they had mild cases of elephantiasis.

The Japanese cherries apparently like good soil and good drainage, and they develop into nice trees more quickly if they get water in summer. I have observed that my neighbor's trees, which are placed on his lawn where they get water all summer for their mass of almost surface roots, like it there, while my trees, growing over spring bulb beds, are dry all summer and grow very slowly. Japanese cherries require no pruning whatever, in fact resent it. Moreover these cherries are not good for cutting. Once they settle down to flowering, their growth seems to be slowed up and nearly limited to the making of flowering spurs.

Like the crab-apples, Japanese cherries have a fall as well as a spring garden value, not in fruit, but because the leaves of most of them turn beautiful reds and yellows and give us the best imitation of an eastern autumn we can get in our equable climate. In California they would be worth growing for this alone.

DECIDUOUS MAGNOLIAS

The deciduous magnolias are among the latter additions to this garden for they were not commercially available in the twenties when it was started. At that time, the plant quarantine stopped the importation of trees and shrubs for resale, and the western nurserymen had not yet developed their own stocks as they have since done. Because the growing of deciduous flowering trees has only become popular in California gardens within the last couple of decades, there are few fine old specimens here which by their size and innumerable flowers show how desirable they can be; one has to go east of the Alleghanies, say in the suburban area around Philadelphia, to see them.

Taking these Chinese trees in the order of blooming, you will see that the Yulan, Magnolia denudata (M. conspicua), is first, with its large cup-shaped pure white flowers. Two specimen trees, reputed to be over sixty years old, are still to be found in Berkeley. They are at their best in January and early February. Stock is rather scarce, and young plants are somewhat difficult to establish, but a three-foot specimen obtained five years ago is now twice that height and is making a good head. Last spring it had over fifty flowers. My advice is, if you are young, plant it, as it will grow even in our overdry California conditions to a height of twenty-five feet or more, and you will then for years have something to look forward to each January.

Magnolia liliflora (M. purpurea, M. discolor), sometimes confused with the at present unavailable M. obovata, is a large shrub with smaller, narrower flowers, purple outside, white inside. Though I got one several years ago and it is doing fairly well under adverse conditions, it is certainly not indispensable and is far exceeded in beauty by its hybrid children. Over a hundred years ago, there was raised in France a new magnolia, M. denudata being the seed and M. liliflora the pollen parent. This hybrid, named Magnolia Soulangeana, is now doubtless the most widely planted of the family. It starts out as a rather irregular shrub but can be developed into a small tree, though most specimens I have seen have multiple trunks. The flowers are large, in shape generally between the two parents. In various seedling forms which have been distributed, it is possible to get early and late flowering plants with a color range from almost pure white to quite deep red purple on the outside of the petals. There is also a very early rose and white form I have not identified which begins to flower in Berkeley as early as Christmas. I have a nearly white form of Soulangeana (listed variously as Alba Superba and as Amabilis), a lovely pale pink I bought as Alexandrina, and a late midseason deep pink and white of particularly fine form for which I have no name. There seem to be so many gradations in season, color, and form in the seedlings offered as Magnolia Soulangeana that it is really best to make your selection, if possible, when they are in flower.

Quite distinct from typical Soulangeana is a late-flowering

hybrid presumably of the same parents, called M. Lennei, a large bush or small, much and stiffly branched tree, which is said to have been found as an accidental cross in northern Italy. It flowers quite late and is generally at its best in March, when it carries dozens of very large cup- or goblet-shaped flowers, rounder at the base than typical Soulangeanas and white inside, but with the outside solid red purple, a gorgeous thing. It is difficult to secure true to name. Twice I bought plants under the name of Lennei before I got the real thing. They both bore earlier, more numerous but smaller flowers of the shape and color of M. Lennei. I have since identified them as what is generally distributed as M. rustica rubra, certainly not a species, probably a Lennei seedling, of quite enough merit to be grown for itself.

I do not have the wonderful early pink-flowering Hima-layan species, Magnolia Campbellii, which can be seen in Golden Gate Park in San Francisco. It is said to take young plants of this about fifteen years to flower. It is therefore a tree for the younger gardener. As it blooms so early, it would in any case be better adapted to a more frost-free garden than ours. I have, however, a young tree of Magnolia Veitchii, the English-raised hybrid between M. Campbellii and M. denu-data, which bears large flowers of a good pink color. This is not so slow to come into flowering as M. Campbellii. In five years it gave us its first bloom, inferior to M. Campbellii and quite late here, but a good clean pink. It seems to be so strong and upright a grower that it should be given ample space for development.

I claim no expert's knowledge of the culture of these large deciduous magnolias, but I have picked up in my limited ex-perience something I failed to find in books about growing them under our conditions. Plants supplied by California nurseries are almost sure to be grafted, though Toichi Domoto told me his were from cuttings and so were on their own roots. They are generally available only in winter or spring here, and are sent balled. In our garden they have no special soil or preparation of it, merely the usual good large hole much bigger than the balled plant. I have preferred north and east exposures rather than hotter and drier ones, as the flowers last longer there. What English and eastern American writers do not sufficiently stress, because it is unnecessary in climates of summer rain, is that the young trees will grow much better for at least two or three summers if they get a thorough soaking every couple of weeks during our dry season, preferably by leaving a hollow around each one, which can be filled with water, not by surface sprinkling. Sometimes the young plants sulk; the tops will refuse to break out into vigorous growth. In two such cases after trying everything else, I decided they didn't like their location, so I had them moved. In both, by some coincidence the top was broken off in transplanting, fortunately above the graft. Thus replanted they both made strong vigorous new shoots, branching out into wide tops. I thereupon next spring cut down a third sulky plant, without transplanting it, and it responded by a strong upright growth from which in two years a fine large head was developed. Several of our best single-stem trees have been developed in this way.

Even without cutting back, occasional suckers appear above the graft. One of these may be used as suggested to make a new top, or they may be pegged down in summer, and in the succeeding spring layers may be made by partially cutting the stems, burying them about six inches, and keeping them watered for a couple of years until well rooted, when they may be severed and replanted. We now have several nice young magnolias on their own roots from such layers; these must be generously watered while young. If you don't want more plants—we do—then it will be better to remove low suckers and let the growth go into the top. No other pruning, except for shaping, is necessary. Most magnolias do not have naturally beautiful form; they tend to be the vegetable equivalent of the five-by-five human.

As the shrubby deciduous Magnolia stellata does not develop into a tree, its garden use is quite different from those already discussed. I consider it one of the best and most distinct deciduous shrubs, slow growing—not wholly a drawback, because it needs no pruning or restraining—and altogether delightful in spring, when its long narrow fragrant white petals on bare branches justify its name of the starry magnolia. Here it does well without summer watering. The pale pink-flowering form, which we do not have but covet, seems to be a much taller and more slender grower, different enough to justify both.

We propose to continue trying other deciduous magnolias as there is opportunity to get them. Our last addition is M. parviflora (M. Sieboldii), quite different from any of the above in that it flowers in May here after leafing out; its lovely four-inch white flowers with their prominent raspberry-red centers are most attractive. Though in time it can become quite a tree, it seems a slow grower here. It is still, after some years, quite shrubby, and certainly wants summer water to keep it going, but it is easily worth the care.

CHAPTER THREE

DECIDUOUS FLOWERING SHRUBS

ERHAPS because I grew up where the lilacs were the most popular spring-flowering shrubs, I have tried them out pretty thoroughly in this garden. I knew they did passably well in the valleys and foothills of northern California, where winters are colder and summers warmer, and rainfall lasts later than in the Berkeley hills. I would have been satisfied with the success generally achieved, let us say at San Jose, or Santa Rosa, or Placerville, but that degree was not possible. I bought budded plants, as recommended by our leading California nurseryman specializing in lilacs, but they sulked, and never made as good growth as own-root ones right beside them. These rooted offshoots sent me by a friend in Indiana did better, though they had a distressing habit of stooling out into clumps of rather weak growth so that I had lots of lilacs to give away but, like dogs with too many pups, the parents looked undernourished. However, from these I did get, about every alternate year, a few nice panicles, and after the hard freezes of 1932 and 1937 I was able to cut fine bunches of lilacs for the house, where they looked better than on the debilitated bushes. The trouble seemed to be that after cutting them—this was just as good as spring pruning—the dry summer immediately followed, and in spite of some watering, they made only short new growths (inadequate for flowering next spring) instead of the arm-length shoots which develop where a nice warm wet spring or early summer follows.

LILACS OR NOT

I have become discouraged here, but I suspect that if you really want lilacs you will try them, and I think conditions rather than skill will determine your success. If your garden is in almost thermostatically even-temperatured San Francisco or in warmer and drier southern California, your chances are slight. Select the place in your garden which is coldest in winter and, if possible, warm in summer. Whether you use the recommended grafted plants or own-root ones, generally more difficult to get, irrigate them well after flowering, but when a good early summer growth has produced the long shoots desirable for next season's flowers, slow down on watering, and stop it altogether in late summer. If you don't cut the flowers, remove the flowered stems or prune them back immediately after flowering, never later. If own-root plants are grown, keep all suckers off or give them to friends who also want to try lilacs.

My attempts to grow lilacs as I remembered them in the cold eastern gardens of my youth may have been nostalgic, but I can't say the same of my experiments with various other deciduous flowering shrubs. My efforts may have been resistance to the doctrine prevalent, particularly in southern California years ago, that there must be no evidence of winter, no bare branches, in our gardens in that tourist season; perhaps I had a feeling that deciduous shrubs indicate more clearly than evergreens the change of seasons, a phenomenon which I have always watched with interest; or perhaps I have been too susceptible to descriptions of the attractions of shrubs in books, magazines, and catalogs written mainly for those with harsher climates which are unsuitable for growing tender evergreen flowering shrubs. But certainly where spring comes late and quickly, there is a pleasure in watching its advent and the rapid swelling of flower buds. The great burst of bloom from spring-flowering shrubs suggests an awakening after a long satisfying unbroken slumber. If deciduous shrubs are not wholly satisfactory here, it is partly because their development is slow and casual, particularly after very mild winters, more like the gradual return to consciousness of a person who has spent a night of broken sleep. Moreover, they do not have here the advantage of appearing just when winter is hardly gone and most of the garden is still brown and leafless. In their season they have even to compete with evergreens or flowering trees of greater size and distinction.

OTHER SPRING SHRUBS

I tested this by buying a nice plant of Forsythia suspensa var. Fortunei, generally considered, from its more upright growth and larger golden bells, as the best of the family. When it flowers in California, not really first but in midspring, it comes when our gardens have far more spectacular yellows— for example the acacias—and it is hardly noticed. Nor can I say that the shrubby spiraeas are exciting in our garden. Spiraea prunifolia var. plena (bridal wreath) is still here, thinly stooling out and not unattractive in a quiet way with its little white balls of double flowers along bare stems, a foil to the red Japanese quince, but not as appealing as where it is more vigorous and has less noticeable neighbors. This and the later Spiraea cantoniensis (S. Reevesiana), a taller upright shrub with good umbels of white flowers, are now the only ones I grow, and I doubt if anyone would much miss them if they were eliminated. Spiraea Vanhouttei I haven't even tried; if I had not seen too much of it in the east, I might plant it here on the margin of a lawn where its white flowers would be most effective.

Nor are the viburnums as exciting in California as in colder climates. Viburnum Carlesii is a lovely early bloomer to be cherished if you can depend on its being covered with flat heads of pink and white sweet-scented flowers, but here, though I have tried to give it a cool eastern exposure, light summer shade, and water, it has never been hearty or exuberant and is often quite shy in flowering. The same is true of the hybrid, more evergreen, Viburnum Burkwoodii, derived from V. Carlesii and V. utile, with similar sweet-smelling flowers— when you get them. Of the older and later deciduous viburnums we have, as gifts from friends, V. tomentosum, of pleasing ovate leaf and unexciting white flowers in cymes, and V. Opulus var. sterile, the old-fashioned roundheaded snowball or guelder rose, which in California is perhaps most valued for the fine red coloring of its maplelike lobed leaves in fall. Both are of easy culture and persist and bloom well every year on a dry bank facing east. All they ask is pruning when flowering is finished.

QUINCES

As early as any deciduous shrub and much the longest in bloom are the flowering quinces, now (we hope permanently) named Chaenomeles lagenaria, after years of being known as Cydonia japonica or Pyrus japonica, or just japonicas to the average gardener. Botanists now restrict the name Cydonia japonica to a low slow-growing species with orange-scarlet flowers, which I have always known as Cydonia Maulei, not a first choice in the family by any means. When we started this garden, we planted quince along the road and since it grew up, it has effectively dissuaded anyone from trying to make a short cut through it. Until we cut it away, I was always glad there were no innocent children around when the man who read the water meter in its midst told the world what he thought of its thorns. This nice unnamed rose-pink form pleased us so much that we got a fine strong-growing blood-red and later a white form, which is less striking. Walter Clarke has now for some years been raising seedlings from various C. lagenaria varieties of distinct growth. I picked out his Rosemary and Enchantress for our garden, but so many of them are new and distinct or of charming color that it is best to make one's own choices.

For central California gardens I think these flowering quinces are by far the most important early deciduous shrubs. Their culture is easy but make up your mind where you want them; though they have always lived through a moving with us, it is evident that this is a shrub which flowers more effectively and is far happier when left in one place for years with pruning confined to the elimination of top or intruding side shoots. Apart from the time japonicas require to get established, they have just one drawback here: the birds sometimes pick off all the flower petals they can reach, and there is nothing you can do about it.

Other deciduous flowering shrubs we have tried and consider worth growing for one reason or another include one native, Ribes sanguineum, the deep pink or red flowering California currant, shabby in summer, but so sweet and so early in flowering that it has some claim to an inconspicuous place. Kerria japonica, in its double form only, will give variety with its little orange balls of flowers, effective when it has stooled out into a clump, best planted in partial shade. For the small garden there is the so-called Japanese flowering almond, Prunus glandulosa, generally available in either pink or white double forms.

TREE PEONIES AND DOGWOOD

Tree peonies are of course deciduous shrubs of midspring flowering. After a visit to Toichi Domoto's wonderful collection at Hayward, I was tempted to add still another specialty for, properly selected and grown, the peonies produce wonderful individual flowers; their culture is not difficult, consisting of ordinary soil with good feeding and autumn setting-out, unless plants are supplied in cans or pots. But though I coveted the huge flowers of the lovely white, pink, and red varieties derived from the old Chinese Paeonia Moutan (P. suffruticosa) and the newer yellow ones from P. lutea, I decided they were for someone with fewer spring specialties, a level garden, and a more formal layout in general.

I have also refrained from such intriguing things as the eastern Cornus florida, the flowering dogwood of the Atlantic coast, which a few of my friends have flowered nicely— some years—as they could give it the cool place and moisture such eastern natives usually demand. Our own native Cornus Nuttallii, from higher, colder, and wetter places than our coastal gardens, is best left at home, though we covet it for its white and green bracts in spring and its crimson foliage in autumn.

WEIGELAS

The most colorful of midseason deciduous shrubs are the weigelas, those eastern Asiatic shrubs formerly but, I understand now, incorrectly called diervilleas. As plants they have little grace. When leafless, their brown twiggy growths are upright and uncompromising while their leaves are dry, coarse, and uninteresting, but for the short time in midspring when they are in flower, the weigelas do give pleasing clumps of pink, rose, red, or white from the funnel-shaped flowers carried gracefully in clusters all along the branches then bending under their weight. I have never grown either Weigela rosea (Diervillea florida), the commonest variety and a quite effective shrub in California, or the dwarfer red Eva Rathke, but of the newer French hybrids I have Ideal and Féerie, respectively described as carmine rose and flesh pink, both quite desirable with larger flowers than the older kinds. I had Majestueux for a while but the lilac rose of its flowers and its uncompromising uprightness lacked appeal for me. I can be tempted, however, to try some new ones like Conquête, the white Mont Blanc, or the peach-pink Le Printemps. The culture of weigelas is easy in any neutral or somewhat alkaline soil. I give them an eastern exposure and aim to prune out the flowering wood after they bloom so as to get strong new canes to carry the next season's flowers, but I have to confess that like most deciduous shrubs they never make the vigorous post-flowering growth here that they do in warmer, wetter summers.

BEAUTY BUSH, MOCK ORANGES, LABURNUM

Related is another Chinese shrub of comparatively recent introduction, Kolkwitzia amabilis, the beauty bush. In the

Pacific Northwest it has disappointed many because it has proved shy flowering under conditions of much moisture and not enough sunshine, and everywhere it seems very slow to get established to the point of blooming. This was certainly true of our specimen, now ten feet high and perhaps as much across, planted facing east, with morning sun and practically no summer watering after the first year. It began flowering three years after planting, and its long arching branches have since been covered every spring with hundreds of pale pink flowers (not unlike smaller weigela blooms), except when it got too tall and I cut it back hard after flowering. Then it took a year off to develop new wood with flower buds. If the bush is left unpruned, the flowers will be succeeded by rather ornamental little brown woolly seed pods. I wouldn't want to be without the beauty bush.

Just as the flowering quinces are my favorites at the opening of spring, I like the hybrid members of the genus Philadelphus to end the season, but they are often as late as June here, and really are early summer bloomers. These mock-oranges do pretty well and the tall, strong, upright-growing French hybrid Virginal, with many large, double white, very sweet-scented flowers, seems particularly happy. We have had half a dozen bushes of it on a dry eastern slope for a dozen years or more without artificial watering or any attention but occasional pruning after flowering. When they got too tall, they were cut down to a couple of feet, and next spring made good new tops, but they missed flowering for lack of young wood the season following this drastic treatment.

We also grow Belle Etoile, a considerably more compact shrub with fragrant single flowers with purple blotches at the base of the petals. For quite a small garden I would suggest the dwarfer, pure white single Manteau d'Hermine, with us well under three feet. I believe any of the Lemoine hybrids preferable to the old-fashioned earlier "syringa," Philadelphus coronarius, which we do not grow but which is the one found in old gardens.

As spring drifts imperceptibly into summer, we have one flowering tree, for it is not a shrub, Laburnum Vossii (L. Watereri), a hybrid which is much finer than the common laburnum or golden chain of English gardens. I cannot forebear mentioning it as it seems to be little grown in California and is such a lovely thing. This relative of the brooms is a tall upright grower, and when in June it is draped with dozens of long racemes of clear yellow pea-shaped flowers it is constantly visited here. It seems to require no special culture.

SUMMER SHRUBS

There are few deciduous shrubs, even in eastern gardens, which flower in summer. In California they seem even rarer. The hybrid deciduous ceanothus raised in France give their flowers mainly in summer. By far the best one is Ceanothus Gloire de Versailles, with powdery blue panicles developing on the new wood. It is quite easy but enjoys summer water as our native ceanothus do not, and it requires heavy spring pruning to keep it in shape and to stimulate the new growth necessary for bloom. There are a number of other varieties, mostly blues, and an odd, dull, pale rose one, Marie Simon, which is quite distinct but has proved a much weaker grower here.

As most gardens are small and many shrubs tend to overcrowd, two summer-flowering ones which can always be kept neat and small are worth noting. Caryopteris incana (C. Mastacanthus) is one of these, with lavender-blue flowers. It is sometimes erroneously called blue spiraea. It comes easily from cuttings and has no cultural peculiarities but needs heavy spring pruning. The other is Ceratostigma Willmottianum, a relative of the shrublet we used to call Plumbago Larpentiae and, like it, bears bright blue flowers on stems a couple of feet high here—an easy thing which can be cut to the ground if it straggles overmuch.

BARBERRIES

If cats were organized into hunt clubs they would subsidize me to refrain from mentioning the terribly thorny deciduous barberries, of which Berberis Thunbergii is best known to eastern gardeners. Though the many newer Chinese species, B. Wilsoniae and B. rubrostilla among them, are of more value where their autumn berries, pink, coral, or red, show against snow or bare branches, I have tried a good many of them in California and raised others, the Wisley hybrids, from seed, but I now doubt if they merit a place in most gardens even for their fall color. Gardeners curse them when they have to be weeded or cut back, for they certainly are spiny.

HYDRANGEAS

The lovely new forms of Hydrangea hortensis (properly H. macrophylla) are of first importance as summer shrubs either in the open or in pots. They should not be confused with that ubiquitous hardy shrub of colder regions, the long-panicled H. arborescens, or its variety grandiflora, rarely seen in California. On the cool coast and where they can be given the regular watering they must have, they should be more widely grown, for they do well and flower profusely in greater shade than most plants endure, and if fed, watered, and pruned the modern varieties will give huge heads of their white, pink, or rose, almost red, sterile flowers. These last many weeks and ultimately fade or dry to decorative greens, pale reds, and purples. They may be cut for indoor use, kept in water for a week or so, and then left quite dry. This shrub, best known in colder climates as a greenhouse or tub plant, is quite hardy where only a few degrees of frost occur, and huge overgrown neglected specimens of weak or indifferent colors are seen in old places. The newer French hybrids are more demanding in care, especially watering, but they are worth it. Unless named varieties can be secured from reputable nurseries, I advise buying these newer hydrangeas in bloom so as to be sure of good colors.

Once acquired, hydrangeas can readily be increased by fall cuttings of the unbloomed season's growth, or in spring by soft tip cuttings of the new growth—the latter better under glass. They like good rich soil and, if left many years in pots, these should be gradually increased in size and a good commercial fertilizer applied occasionally when plants are in a period of growth. Blue hydrangeas are the result of acid soils; by the incorporation of peat in the potting soil and the use of aluminum sulphate both in the soil and as a top dressing, many of the pink and rose varieties can be induced to give heads of blue or rich purple flowers. Personally, I prefer pinks. The all-important requirement of these hydrangeas is water. They should never be allowed to flag for lack of it, especially if they are grown in pots, always in part shade; big pots can take a lot. Open-ground plants need less attention to watering, but even they are greatly improved by regular summer soakings.

CHAPTER FOUR

EVERGREEN SHRUBS

---

*T*HE outstanding characteristic of most California gardens is the presence of evergreen shrubs, not conifers but broad-leaved flowering shrubs, tender in any but the mild climates of the Pacific coast or of the South. As furnishings they have great advantages, for by their use the surroundings of the house can be kept green and cheerful in winter and also remain green in summer when the countryside gets brown. This permanence of foliage, which particularly appeals to the conservative gardener, has many advantages. The broad-leaved shrubs are ideal for plantings around the foundations of the house, masking at all times the rigid line where it joins the ground, tying the house to the ground, and blending it in with the garden. For the boundaries of the property a mixed evergreen shrubbery will provide a permanent screen, not merely one for summer, and the varied textures of the leafage offer a beauty of their own. For flower borders such shrubbery gives clean, green, constant background which can be depended on all through the year. The smaller evergreen shrubs are excellent for framing lawns, where the less drought-resistant ones are particularly happy. In addition, a careful selection of evergreen shrubs can be counted on to give colorful flowers over practically the whole year. In the leanest time, the autumn, it will be the orange or red berries of the evergreen shrubs which will provide a substitute for the bright autumn foliage of colder areas.

One should not generalize about soils or culture. Mention will be made of specific requirements where these exist, but naturally the evergreen shrubs we plant most are those which are easiest to grow here and so require little special knowledge. Most of them are quite adaptable, and a large proportion of the commoner ones are drought-resistant. Because they have no dormant season, bare root planting or transplanting is not satisfactory. Plants are always supplied in pots or in the lowly tin cans, which have many advantages in that they are expendable and less subject to evaporation. Our experience has been all in favor of buying young—and therefore relatively inexpensive—plants just ready for a shift from their containers, rather than larger pot-bound ones or big open-ground specimens which must lose many roots in the necessary balling for shipment. A small plant in a good large hole full of loose soil, well watered and cared for, will often outstrip the bigger one which seemed so much more imposing at the beginning. While gardeners never will be persuaded to let things stay put—they would lose too much of the fun of changing or improving the garden if they did—they will save themselves some grief and much work if they plant as many evergreen shrubs as possible where they are going to remain.

Propagation of these shrubs is sometimes by seed, sometimes by cuttings, but the average gardener can well afford to buy the plants he wants, though mention will occasionally be made of means of increase. Cultivation, removal of weeds, and watering are the main tasks of growing. In large places the ground is just lightly dug between shrubs once a year, in spring. Watering should be occasional and thorough rather than a matter of frequent sprinkling; more watering is necessary when plants are young than when they are well established and the developed root system can go deeper for moisture. Pruning is largely a matter of controlling too exuberant growth or of shaping the plant, and much of it may be done at the convenience of the gardener, though naturally the time after flowering is likely to be preferable.

The number and variety of evergreen shrubs which will do well in California are bewildering. To discuss them all would require a book larger than this one, so I can give only a selection, mainly of those which I have grown at some time and believe to have merit. Not all will appeal to any one gardener and a number which may have done so may not be found here. In the two succeeding chapters some special evergreen shrubs are given place by themselves.

SHRUBS FOR WINTER AND SPRING

Though seasons overlap to a degree, I shall discuss general groupings of winter and spring, of summer and fall flowering shrubs. In winter and spring come very desirable California natives, all sufficiently hardy to occur in the wild and therefore likely to do well in our gardens, provided we remember that California natives get no summer rain and do not want it; they should be planted where summer watering will leave them out. None are more important than the ceanothus, the so-called wild lilacs of our chaparral. From the numerous species * I select C. arboreus, the Catalina ceanothus, as the earliest, really a small tree, suitable for boundaries or backgrounds, and

* Thoroughly described by Van Rensselaer and McMinn in *Ceanothus*, published by the Santa Barbara Botanic Garden in 1942.

covered in January or February with clusters of pale blue flowers. My favorite, however, and it is a midspring bloomer, would be C. impressus, the Santa Barbara ceanothus, a densely branched shrub, from three to five feet tall and of the same breadth, with small dark green crinkled foliage, always attractive, and covered in March or April with panicles of bright blue flowers—by all odds the most striking bit of color in the garden in its season. The San Diego ceanothus, C. cyaneus, is taller, up to ten feet, and later, flowering here in early May with large clusters of medium blue flowers, a fine thing but apparently shorter-lived in gardens than most of the family.

Dendromecon rigida, the tree poppy, I have seen growing wild on hot dry gravelly banks along the road between Santa Maria and Lompoc, in bloom there in February, later here, with gray-green leaves and canary-yellow poppylike flowers. This shrub, which is a rather scraggly grower, up to about ten feet, must have good drainage and does not like much summer water. I lost mine, probably because of our heavy retentive soil, but it is worth trying again.

Fremontia californica is one of the most striking of our native shrubs, flowering in late spring in the foothills of the Sierras, growing often on warm rocky slopes in thin soil where, as on the road from Red Bluff to Mineral, fine stands may be seen, the not very graceful shrubs covered with deep yellow bowl-shaped flowers. I have grown only the southern form, F. Californica var. mexicana, which under garden conditions tends to develop into a rather gaunt and awkward small tree. Its deep yellow flowers have rust-colored bases. Besides offering a big show in spring, it blooms scatteringly thereafter. It needs replacing since, when old, it tends to blow over in winter, if it is growing where the ground is very wet, or to die off from other causes.

Carpenteria californica is a much neater shrub, erect, five feet or more high, with long narrow green foliage and many clusters of white flowers in late spring, resembling the old syringa. Carpenteria gets shabby after flowering, due to leaf curl from aphis infestation, which I am told can be controlled by spraying as soon as it appears. Give this shrub full sun, but it will stand more summer water than most natives.

This year we have added the fuchsia-flowered gooseberry, Ribes speciosum, to our few native shrubs, in part for its early red flowers but also because of its attractive foliage, evergreen in cultivation, and its good general effect as a specimen shrub a couple of feet high. It suckers and is very spiny. Being a coast-range plant it is easy to grow.

SHRUBS FROM AUSTRALIA

Most of our imported evergreen shrubs have been brought from climates somewhat like ours. From the antipodes and especially from Australia come many of these shrubs and trees as well, the eucalyptus and acacia among them. In our early years we were intrigued by the large tree acacia, A. decurrens var. mollis (A. mollissima), the Australian green wattle, with feathery green foliage and large sprays of yellow, very sweet-scented flowers in spring, and also by the smaller, earlier, gray-foliaged A. Baileyana, still occasionally planted, but these are just too vigorous, too weedy for most gardens, and should be restricted to large places. There are also a host of smaller shrub-like acacias, quick, easy, and drought-resistant, but they too seem to have lost favor.

But from Australia come some very desirable small shrubs,

among them Chorizema ilicifolium (C. cordatum), almost re-
cumbent, with pleasant but prickly edged leaves and racemes
of pea-shaped orange and magenta flowers, a striking and attractive combination. Chorizema likes the sun and is a little
tender, so is best for gardens with mild winters. The Australian correas are relatively little grown for such attractive small
shrubs, but C. pulchella, a winter bloomer with dainty pink
hanging bell-shaped flowers, is quite hardy and can be recommended for small gardens. So can the one grevillea which
seems so suitable for them but is rarely found, Grevillea rosma-
rinifolia, from New South Wales, a happily slow-growing
shrub, now after ten years about six feet high here. Its very
narrow linear foliage is always good, and all winter and spring
its unusual light red long-lasting flowers cause comment here
—all favorable. It is hardy and easy.

From New Zealand come the leptospermums best adapted
to our gardens, forms of Leptospermum scoparium, a narrow-
leaved white-flowered shrub, going here up to ten or twelve
feet in time. The type is rarely grown, but Nichollsii a red-
flowered form with bronzy red leaves, is highly decorative in
late spring, and other color variations are appearing, such as
the pink form commonly called Chapmannii. But my choice
would be the recently imported variety, Keatleyi, with much
freer growth and white rose-centered flowers, far larger than
any other form; it blooms all winter and is a really fine shrub.
There is also a pale pink double variety of L. scoparium, and
from breeding done at the University of California, Los
Angeles, by Dr. W. E. Lammerts we may soon expect a whole
series of lovely double colored forms. English gardeners wax
enthusiastic over the New Zealand olearias or tree asters, small
shrubs which apparently like a damper climate than ours.

Olearia stellulata (O. Gunniana) from seed gave a few plants which I thought might take the place here of the herbaceous perennial asters, but they languished and most of them died out.

The pittosporums are my last nominations of spring-flowering antipodeans. They are large shrubs, submitting readily to pruning. Pittosporum eugenoides and P. tenuifolium (P. nigricans) from New Zealand, and P. undulatum, the Victorian box from Australia, are best known as materials for tall broad evergreen hedges, though the last makes a beautiful free-flowering white tree in sections where it is hardy. As a flowering shrub, the quite easy and hardy P. tobira, the Japanese pittosporum, is grown particularly for its neat habit and fragrant white flowers.

SOUTH AFRICAN SHRUBS

From South Africa come a couple of good small shrubs. Aster fruticosus (Diplopappus fruticulosus) breaks all the rules for asters as it is a spring-flowering evergreen shrub of two or three feet, its rosy mauve flowers suggestive of some Michaelmas daisies. Like most South Africans, it loves the sun and is not fussy about being watered. It can take several degrees of frost but was killed here in the hard winter of 1937. However, it is easily propagated by cuttings. Diosma ericoides (breath of heaven) is a small, up to two feet, heathlike shrub with myriads of little white flowers. It is valued for its neat habit and fragrant foliage as well as for its bloom. It prefers an acid soil with leaf mold or peat in it.

It is, however, the ericas or heathers which are the most appreciated contribution of South Africa to our group of winter- or spring-flowering shrubs. By far the easiest and most frequently grown in California is what nurserymen list as Erica melanthera, but which our authority on this family, Eric Walther, says is properly E. canaliculata, a vigorous species, generally about five feet high, having large sprays of little lilac-pink flowers with black-tipped anthers. This has been much grown in northern California, and the cut branches are shipped east in bloom to be sold as Scotch heather. Since E. canaliculata is less fastidious about the acidity of the soil than other ericas and since it flowers in midwinter, often as early as Christmas, it doubtless justifies its first place. The other spring-blooming South African heaths which I have grown are E. hirtiflora (E. regerminans) and E. subdivaricata (E. persoluta). These very different species were attractive, but we lost them, probably because they required a sandy, peaty, or acid soil and we did not have it, though a sour or acid character could have been produced by incorporating dusting sulphur or aluminum sulphate in the soil. The large-flowered summer-blooming South African heathers—Jubilee and President Felix Faure are examples—are lovely things but too temperamental for most busy general gardeners.

Some easier winter- and spring-flowering heathers from the Mediterranean countries, though secondary in beauty, also are grown in California. These are E. mediterranea, which I dislike because it holds its dead florets, and E. australis from Spain, which is better. For the much taller, dull white-flowered E. arborea, its better white hybrid, E. Veitchii, is a good substitute.

SHRUBS FROM THE MEDITERRANEAN

Coming to European, actually Mediterranean, shrub importations, we find that Viburnum tinus, the evergreen laurestinus of old gardens, is the first to flower, with flat cymes of pink-budded white flowers appearing as early as January. It is very easy and happy here, nice enough in its better forms and tough enough for hedge use, but somehow without the charm or the fragrance of its temperamental deciduous relative, V. Carlesii. Other old friends from the south of Europe are rosemary and germander, plants of sentiment and of aromatic fragrance, but of limited garden value. Rosmarinus officinalis is the botanical name of the former, a six-foot narrow-leaved shrub with small lavender flowers in winter. I grow only the prostrate form now and have eliminated Teucrium fruticans, the germander, though this casual gray-leaved blue-flowered shrub is nice enough; one just hasn't room or time for everything. I was sorry to lose the last of the shrubs to be mentioned here, a gray-leaved shrubby morning-glory, Convolvulus cneorum, but as it comes easily from cuttings, I will get it again, for it is always neat and pleasant even without its spring bloom of white funnel-shaped flowers—a good plant, especially for the small garden.

From Asia, we get Daphne odora, the three- or four-foot evergreen which is so cherished for its sweet yet pungent flowers, in late winter—if you get them. When our garden was new and its location was sunnier, we always had lots of flowers from this daphne; now, perhaps because of shade, it has become very shy, and I confess I do not know how to help this, other than by trying to see what moving it would do. At least we can still depend on another white-flowered fragrant winter bloomer, Osmanthus Delavayi, which does well beside our front door facing southwest—its neat dark green foliage, not unlike box, and its unobtrusive habit fitting the entrance to this simple house. Still another neat and slower-growing oriental shrub for the small garden is Raphiolepis ovata, compact, with dark green leathery leaves and fragrant white flowers in spring, a low shrub, often used because it doesn't need pruning to prevent overrunning its neighbors.

From the western hemisphere we have enjoyed three good evergreens. Abutilon vitifolium from Chile is a tall shrub, almost a tree, with a rather untidy habit, evergreen vinelike leaves, and much larger, flatter blue flowers in spring than one gets from the smaller but better-known flowering maples. Give it, or its less desirable white form, not too prominent a place, well back of a path. Berberis Darwinii, from the same country, is an evergreen barberry with pleasing dark green spiny foliage and racemes of orange flowers in winter or spring, followed in fall by inconspicuous black berries. This is another possible hedge plant of informal character, though its hybrid, B. stenophylla, is probably superior for impenetrability, if otherwise a less pleasing plant. Both are easy and extend themselves by suckers which can be used to start new plantings. The last of this ABC group from south of us is Choisya ternata, the Mexican orange, whose broad-leaved rounded form and panicles of white fragrant flowers persuaded many that it should get the doorside place so often given to Spiraea Vanhouttei in the east. Its culture is easy, but it is subject to a smut or scale which sometimes disfigures it and has perhaps been responsible for its decline in popularity.

FLOWERS FOR SUMMER AND AUTUMN

From the evergreen shrubs which contribute most to the garden in summer and autumn I shall first mention a few which are desirable for their summer flowers and then some of the berry-bearing shrubs to close the year.

I would not want to be without abelias. The Mexican species, Abelia floribunda, is not yet widely distributed though it is the most showy of the family, with brilliant flowers of bright rosy purple in hanging clusters in late spring or early summer. It is only moderately hardy and likes water in summer, a sunny place in cool gardens or half shade in warm ones, and neutral or acid soil. We also grow the later A. Schumannii, a more drought-resistant Chinese species, with pink flowers, a little suggestive of a dwarfer, three- to five-foot beauty bush. Our first choice, however, has always been the hybrid A. grandiflora, with glossy green leaves, restrained growth—resembling some fuchsias—and rosy white flowers for months in summer. Its easy adaptability to almost all conditions and its great resistance to drought particularly endear it to busy gardeners.

The abutilons or flowering maples are best known as pot plants, but as they are quite hardy in California they can be grown outdoors, in semishade preferably, where their bell-shaped flowers will be carried all summer and into autumn. Besides the larger hybrids—readily raised from seed or by cuttings and giving a nice range of colors—there is a tough, more drought-resistant species, A. megapotamicum, with distinct red flowers, and a hybrid called Eclipse, of the same character but mainly in orange. These are very easy open-ground plants.

The cestrums, tall quick-growing shrubs with evergreen lilaclike leaves, I might have overlooked were not Cestrum aurantiacum now in full flower here in mid-July, its drooping terminal clusters of buff-orange flowers unusual and appreciated. This Guatemalan species demands little and grows here in semishade, spreading by offsets and seed. I prefer it to the taller, somewhat lax and climbing red-flowered C. elegans (C.

purpureum, also called Habrothamnus elegans) which flowers almost continuously.

The daboecias or Irish heaths came late into our life, but now they are grown and enjoyed here where we want dwarf neat shrubs with small green leaves and summer flowers. These they give in either purple, pink, or white, very graceful, nodding, and in terminal clusters. The Irish heaths prefer an acid soil with such water as they get from proximity to a lawn. They should be used more in small cool gardens.

The older escallonias, a husky if somewhat coarse South American species, like the white Escallonia montevidensis or the crimson E. rubra, used to be grown more in our gardens, but they are really best in big places or in parks or parkings. Mainly from Irish breeding of other hardier species, we now have a series of equally vigorous, adaptable, far more slender-growing, smaller-flowered and earlier-blooming—June—hybrids, which are better for most gardens. Donard seedling with white flowers, Edinensis, a rosy pink, and C. F. Ball, a crimson, are typical, and from California breeding we are likely to get other improvements. Escallonias come readily from cuttings, are quite drought-resistant, and would make good informal hedge plantings. They naturally grow up to ten feet or more but can be kept lower by drastic pruning.

The shrubby veronicas of New Zealand, now classified as hebes, after their appearance at the San Francisco Exposition of 1915, had some popularity in the cooler, foggier sections to which they were adapted. They varied greatly in habit from such trailers as Hebe chathamica and H. Traversii, one foot, up to and beyond the five-foot H. speciosa; many like H. cupressoides had foliage suggestive of other plants. They are interesting to collect—any cutting will root—and they can be clipped for low hedges. But they are now less popular, and for most gardens the one with the most attractive flowers, H. Hulkeana (Veronica Hulkeana), would be enough; it grows to three feet and has long sprays of lovely lavender flowers, far more attractive than the stiff spikes of most members of the family.

Also less popular than they once were are the dwarf lantanas, not quite hardy enough for northern California but almost too happy in the south. Unlike the climbers and trailers these are not difficult to keep in bounds and even can be clipped for hedges. They have no cultural demands, enjoy heat like Mexicans, and are useful plants even if a trifle on the plebeian side.

Two more facile flowering shrubs—actually subshrubs which can be cut to the ground each year—are Lavatera Olbia, a casual but easily satisfied mallow from southern Europe, with lilac-pink single flowers, and the African Leonotis Leonurus, popularly called lions-ear or lions-tail, growing three or four feet high, with long brilliant orange flowers in whorls at the top of each branch to compensate for a somewhat untidy habit. Do not plant these two shrubs together as their colors clash violently.

No California garden with a fair amount of sunshine and warmth should be without lavenders. There are a number of species of secondary importance of which I grow a Spanish one, Lavandula Stoechas, spring-flowering, with dark purple flowers and bracts, quite dwarf, quite ornamental, but without the scent or sentiment of the common lavender, L. officinalis (L. Spica or L. vera). This is a gray-leaved subshrub, up to three feet, which can be kept lower by pruning, a summer bloomer, its color, of course, lavender. It is the flowers, when dried, which are so fragrant and so much used for perfume.

I now grow only a dwarfer compact form which I raised from the seed an English friend sent me from her garden. It would make a nice hedge and so would the taller type, if properly pruned after flowering.

Tibouchina semidecandra is the new approved name of what has more commonly been called Pleroma splendens, a tall upright summer- and fall-flowering shrub, up to ten feet high, with velvety veined leaves and gorgeous deep blue-purple flowers, three inches across. It is not very hardy but has stood every winter in Berkeley since 1937, when it was pretty well frozen back. It likes a warm place but will stand some shade, though the best specimens I have seen get all morning sun from facing east. Tibouchina semidecandra is worth anyone's growing.

There are of course many other flowering evergreen shrubs and trees which cannot be considered here. I have preferred to write of those I have grown, hence the omission of such wonderfully colored and perfumed small flowering shrubs, sometimes trees, as the oleanders (Nerium Oleander) which in warm places and especially in southern California bloom all summer and can be found in both single and double forms in a range of color which includes white, pink, salmon, and rose— good shrubs for private gardens, as well as for planting along drives or in parkings.

BERRY-BEARING SHRUBS

Berry-bearing shrubs, mainly cotoneasters and pyracanthas in newer species or varieties, have provided our autumn, even our winter gardens with yellows and reds which were quite lacking two or three decades ago. While there are other shrubs which can contribute fall berries, our native Toyon or Christmas berry has a tendency to disease disfigurements, and with aralias the larger proportion of foliage to berries makes them less effective than other shrubs chosen for their emphasis on berries. Even among these much selection will be necessary. It should also be noted that botanically pyracanthas used to be considered cotoneaster species; they are now separated.

In selecting cotoneasters for fall color, little attention need be paid in California to the deciduous species, and no space will be given here to the prostrate forms, which are mainly of value as ground covers or rock garden subjects. By far the most commonly grown species is Cotoneaster pannosa, a small-leaved shrub, ten feet high or more, with arching branches which reduce the effect of height, give it grace, and show off its red berries. It is inexpensive, coming up freely from self-sown seed, persistent, and easy to grow without any watering after it is established. Its berries, though of good color, are not as numerous or as bright as one might like, and they are beloved by robins, which clear them off rapidly after heavy snow occurs in the Sierras. My first choice of the tall evergreen cotoneasters is C. Parneyi, which has larger, greener leaves and larger, deeper red berries in bigger clusters than other varieties; its spring flowers too, though not exciting, are quite the most attractive of any of the cotoneasters I have grown.

Pyracanthas—the old common name is firethorn—lack the grace of growth of the cotoneasters, having stiff upright or horizontal branches, and as their popular name indicates, they have thorns which at least fit them for hedges. Apart from such use, their uncompromising habit makes most of them more suitable for training against walls or planting in groups by themselves than for the mixed shrubbery plantings into which cotoneasters can be blended. As their orange-red berries persist, keep them away from pink-flowering trees or shrubs or take the color consequences.

Of the older pyracanthas most gardens could hardly use more than one, the orange-berried Pyracantha coccinea var. Lalandii, a very vigorous grower with the largest, most persistent berries. For a while its place was contested by P. angustifolia, but the sad susceptibility of that species to pear blight has practically eliminated it. Another, with smaller orange berries borne all along the slender willowy branches, I got from Walter Clarke of San Jose under the name P. rogersiana aurantiaca, a firethorn which is apparently the same one the Armstrong Nurseries in southern California list as P. crenulata rogersiana. With both of them I agree that it is worth growing for its spring bloom alone, for I never saw any shrubs so completely covered as ours with lovely lacy white flowers; it is reputed to be immune to pear blight. There are a number of fine red-berried pyracanthas with somewhat confused nomenclature. My first choice has been one listed as P. formosiana var. splendens (which Bailey calls P. Koidzumii) or for P. crenato-serrata var. Graberi, a very vigorous form with huge clusters of big bright crimson berries, a finer form than the variety generally sent out as yunnanensis.

HEDGE PLANTS

Questions are often asked about evergreen hedge plants in California. In years past, the hungry and malodorous privet was much used as was also Monterey cypress along the coast, but if big tall hedges must be had, the pittosporums or, in warm gardens, Eugenia myrtifolia will do a far better job. For a low hedge I prefer Lonicera nitida, easy, enduring drastic pruning and coming readily from cuttings. Myrtus communis and the smaller hebes, or boxwood, if you can get and afford it, are other possibilities. For informal screens and impediments to passage, Japanese quinces, pyracanthas, fuchsias, the taller cistus, and borders of mixed shrubs are effective and may be more interesting and less work than clipped hedges.

CHAPTER FIVE

SUN ROSES, ROCK ROSES, BROOMS

$\mathcal{S}$ UN ROSES, rock roses, and brooms may be said to belong to my Mediterranean period, that decade or so of my gardening life when, tired of fighting nature, of trying to grow things which preferred cold winters and wet summers, I turned to the tough drought-resistant shrubs and subshrubs of the countries around the Mediterranean where the climate is more like that of California than of eastern North America. My interest began when I learned that the helianthemums or sun roses, so often winter-killed on the Atlantic coast, survived lesser cold and greater drought here and were clean and green all the year round in our rock garden. When I had a larger garden, I naturally turned to their big brothers, the rock roses, members of the genus Cistus. In the last phase of my Mediterranean period, the emphasis was on the botanically unrelated brooms, genista or cytisus, horticulturally happy along with the helianthemums and cistus, because of their comparable drought-resistance.

Though I have had some lifelong loves, my progress as a gardener seems to have shown some inconstancy, an inclination to enthusiastically collect and cultivate certain plants and later to drop or, more often, taper off my emphasis on them. During the gathering, no trouble for me (or my friends) was too great if it gave me a chance to grow or try out species or varieties of the family then under study. Later, during the dispersal, I would discontinue growing all but outstanding members. This is the present situation regarding sun roses, rock roses, and brooms.

SUN ROSES

In our first small Berkeley hillside garden we found helianthemums useful and ornamental in the rock garden, to cover its winter nakedness with fine green or gray evergreen foliage; they would submit to any pruning, and provided this occurred before spring, the plants would be covered with great numbers of small colorful flowers like single roses in April and May, with occasional bloom in summer and fall. The flowers are fugitive, however, lovely in and as the morning, but gone by noon on sunny days. In this the varieties differ, some retaining their flowers till late afternoon, particularly in cool foggy weather. All sun roses are apparently forms of Helianthemum nummularium (formerly H. vulgare). Some have small, very narrow green leaves, others have larger leaves of a shinier green; some have quite gray foliage. In growth some are neat and compact, others are lax and casual so that they need occasional clipping to keep good form. They never spread too much, as the branches do not root as they go, but small pieces taken in summer or fall and put in a sandy propagating bed in semi-shade will readily root and can then be potted or even planted out. Sun roses do not enjoy moving when they have become large or long established—a very human attitude. For many years, in fact until rather recently, I thought they could endure the summer season without any watering, but it has become evident that without some care and irrigation they will be unsatisfactory and short-lived.

I started by getting what forms I could find in nurseries and catalogs. Then, from seed secured from English and Scotch amateurs, hundreds of plants were raised, some of the best of which I later propagated by cuttings. Two outstanding ones were introduced, a very large white, variously offered in nurseries as St. Mary's, or Notre Dame—after all, the same thing— and a fine orange named California. More important, however, was a set of fine English varieties which I imported and made available to California gardeners, such excellent forms as the vigorous large-flowered yellow Goldilocks, the fine-colored but somewhat lax crimson American Beauty, Jersey Cream, and Jock Scot Improved, the last a good brick red. The best collections are in the nurseries of the Pacific Northwest. Where compact plants are preferred, it is best to select from the Scotch varieties of the Ben series, like Ben Nevis; they are most suitable for small rock gardens. Though I have now stopped collecting sun roses and don't think them as happy under neglect as I once did, I still believe them most desirable shrublets for rock gardens and edgings.

In the late twenties and thirties I also collected some very different species of Helianthemum, on the whole far taller, rangier, generally gray-leaved shrubs, since reclassified as a group under the name Halimium. I acquired a neat little shrub with small yellow flowers, now called Halimium alyssoides (then Helianthemum alyssoides), which was never too vigorous here even when regularly watered. Much huskier and more persistent has been the white-flowered Halimium umbellatum (formerly Helianthemum umbellatum), a dark narrow-leaved trailer which now covers a couple of square feet and would crowd its neighbors further if allowed. It is worth while for the large rock garden. But it is really the big tall grayish-leaved members of the family which are most important for wherever you want such shrubs. They are a bit dry-looking, but they do have the merit of being drought-resistant here, and their round inch-wide yellow flowers are quite distinct and pleasant and effective on spring mornings when the plants are covered with bloom, but they too are fugitive, so the value of these halimiums is in an easy tolerance of drought and neglect. If I had space for only one, I think I would pick Halimium lasianthum (formerly Helianthemum formosum). It is perhaps two feet in height, extending by top growth, not rooting, so that an individual plant may eventually spread over four to six feet of ground. It is covered on spring mornings with attractive flat yellow flowers, each petal having a brown spot at the base. One without spots appeared in a lot of seedlings I raised years ago. My second choice would be Halimium ocymoides (formerly Helianthemum ocymoides), a taller three- to four-foot lankier shrub with similar yellow, dark-spotted, single roselike flowers. Its main season of bloom is late spring, but there are occasional flowers in late summer and fall. The taller, larger, much grayer-leaved Halimium halimifolium is more important for its gray foliage effect, like Atriplex, than for its somewhat larger but sparser yellow flowers. All may be raised from seed or propagated from cuttings in late summer or early autumn, say August or September, when half-ripened tips of the season's growth have always rooted readily for me in a sandbox. A local nurseryman tells me he has failed when he tried them at other seasons.

ROCK ROSES

It is, however, the rock roses or cistuses which are still pretty prevalent on our hillside. They were often in mind, oddly enough, during the war. Reference to the Maquis or French irregulars reminded us that they took their name from the wild shrubbery of the French Mediterranean area, which presumably sheltered them. This maquis, or growth of drought-resistant evergreens, corresponds to our Californian chaparral, and various species of cistus are its chief constituents, just as the wild lilac or ceanothus constitutes much of ours.

After growing many of the white-flowered species, I have decided I can get along nicely with three quite distinct ones. The first, Cistus corbariensis, a hybrid, I pick as the best of the small-flowered whites, a shrub of reasonably restrained habit, over three feet high unpruned, with nice dark green foliage and pink flower buds which make it quite as attractive just before blooming as when its myriads of neat single roselike flowers cover it every morning for weeks in late spring. Being a hybrid, it has to be propagated by cuttings, but these root readily in a sandbox in late summer. Much less attractive but quite distinct is C. laurifolius, a somewhat stiff shrub with dark laurel-like foliage, rather funereal in winter, but with fairly large white flowers and much later in season of blooming. Its great advantage is its hardiness in climates colder than ours. It is difficult to root from cuttings but comes easily and, of course, true from seed.

Concerning Cistus ladaniferus a good deal of confusion has existed in California. Probably because it was tender in England, this tall erect narrow-leaved species with large attractive white flowers, each petal having a conspicuous red-brown spot at its base, was often replaced (under the same name) by a hardier hybrid which is properly C. cyprius. This also has white flowers, smaller ones, with the typical spots, but in the substituted hybrid they appear in clusters while in the true C. ladaniferus they are borne singly; C. cyprius also has broader and less sticky leaves. I have had this hybrid several times, and it always dies young, and not because it is good, for its parent is preferable for permanence and size. Cistus ladaniferus is a bit hard to propagate by cuttings but comes very easily from seed. Among the plants I raised from imported seed appeared the pure white form, which is easily the largest and most striking white. Oddly enough, this variety often holds its flowers for a couple of days, certainly an advantage when most cistus bloom is fugitive. It grows six feet or more. I am now interested in a new species, C. Palhinhaii, which recently received an Award of Merit from the Royal Horticultural Society when it was shown by its discoverer, Collingwood Ingram. It is described as "a very attractive species of dwarf, spreading habit from south-west Portugal. It bears plenty of round milk-white flowers which measure three inches across and have a fascinating little cluster of bright yellow stamens." Its possible use as a ground cover so intrigued me that I wrote Mr. Ingram for seed and now have a dozen nice plants on a steep bank where they should flower next spring.

Turning to the pink-flowered rock roses, one has to acknowledge that Nature has not been very discriminating in the shade of pink or rose she has provided, the former being frequently of the cold or bluish pinks and the latter near the despised magenta. I began my collection of pink cistus with C. villosus and its variety C. villosus creticus. They still provide a fine gray-green ground cover for a good deal of the steep never-watered bank facing our front door. The dark green crinkly Cistus crispus, which I also raised from seed, was a good ground cover and its red-purple flowers were not unpleasant in color, but it seems to have disappeared in a spring cleaning we made three years ago to find room for irises. I can live without it. The only pink species of good clear color I have seen is C. parviflorus, a small slower-growing, quite gray-leaved shrub with inch-wide clear pink flowers. It is distinct in any collection, but is very difficult to root from cuttings.

The only good pinks and rose reds are hybrids and therefore to be propagated by cuttings. In the deeper color range is Cistus purpureus (a chance hybrid apparently of C. ladaniferus and C. villosus), and here we have one of the very best and easiest of all flowering evergreen drought-resistant shrubs. Though it originated in southern France over a hundred years ago, it was introduced to California (by Golden Gate Park) only a few years ago and then was listed by California nurserymen as a novelty, which it was to them. It has good dark green foliage and deep rose-red (not purple in the popular use of that word) flowers, with deeper spots at the base of the petals, a character derived from C. ladaniferus. It roots very readily and will make a flowering plant in less than a year. With us it grows four to five feet high and must be restrained by pruning if it has near neighbors. Silver Pink, a chance hybrid found in an English nursery, we imported at great pains. It is like a lovely wild rose in color, but the plant has proved a disappointing grower here, tending to get dry and shabby in summer and quite occasionally to die out. I suspect it wants more summer water and care than we give it, judging from one plant I still have which seems happier since it accidentally got irrigation. This year I added plants of a newer but similar chance hybrid, Doris Hibberson, from Victoria, B. C. Its flowers are almost identical with Silver Pink, just a shade deeper, quite pure in color, and its growth and gray foliage seem decidedly better in its first summer with us. It may replace Silver Pink.

The rock roses have proved useful in my garden because in one sense—and one only—I am an isolationist; that is, I like some space between me and my neighbors. But without the means to care for this space in an expensive way, good, easy, drought-resistant ground covers seem the solution, and these are most often found among shrubs from Mediterranean climates—our own California climate and those of southern Europe, certain parts of Australia, South Africa, and the west coast of South America. As we tend to get our ideas of the cultural needs of such shrubs from the adventurous English gardeners, who will try anything, especially if it is hard for them, we are occasionally misled. For example, full sunlight is invariably recommended for all cistus, but many of them form forest undergrowth in their sunnier native climes, and naturally here they will also accept shade, though in foggier coastal gardens I am sure they will stand full sunshine equally well. The impression also seems to exist that they are difficult to transplant. In spring or fall we have been invariably successful in moving them. Last spring we literally wrenched out, bare root, from a wire-bottomed propagating bed some more than a year old plants of C. corbariensis and C. purpureus, and hardly any died when planted in the garden. Furthermore, we moved dozens of self-sown seedlings of C. ladaniferus last April and May, some two feet high, and didn't lose one. A further impression seems to be that they will not stand drastic pruning, but last spring we were under the necessity of either digging out or pruning to the ground a lot of old self-sown plants of several species, and we chose the latter alternative. Now, six months later, they are covered with new growth from the base and look in the best of health. Last I can add that we have ample evidence of their happiness here, for nearly all the species grown have freely self-sown and come up in a stiff soil by no means hospitable to most plants in the baby stage.

BROOMS

When this garden had little shade, plenty of drought, and about as much sunshine as one gets hereabouts, we grew so many brooms that we might almost have been called Plantagenets like the early English royal house which had the broom or *Planta genista* for its emblem. The brooms have not proved as drought-resistant or as permanent as the rock roses, probably because many of them come from well north of the Mediterranean, but it was an interesting experiment to try all those we could get. Those remaining today attest to the value we feel some brooms have for the decoration of gardens. We tried almost all those of good repute. Some species proved of merely botanical interest, and those I shall hardly mention. Most of the others are still in the garden, though less dominant than a decade ago. As it is necessary to look at the seed to distinguish between the two great broom families of cytisus and genista, I shall disregard botanical distinctions and consider first the dwarfs, then those of medium height, and last the tall ones.

We had at one time a good many brooms that were either quite flat or little shrublets suitable to rock gardens, but only three species and one hybrid are still with us. Genista dalmatica, a drought-resistant Mediterranean plant, is a pleasant but unexciting thing to cover a little slope or fall over a rocky ledge, but its good green foliage and yellow flowers, pea-shaped as with all brooms, are not so striking that we would miss it greatly if it left us. I would more regret Cytisus Ardoinii, a low but upright little plant from the mountains of the French Riviera, as I like to see it covered with yellow flowers every April and it is well-mannered and never crowds out others. It has slowly increased, however, since we planted it a dozen years ago. It is easy and apparently permanent and propagates readily from cuttings. Genista hispanica, the Spanish gorse, is one of those low, round, little pincushionlike shrubs with leaves so spiny that our cat is never found sitting on it; its deep yellow flowers are perhaps less important than its foliage effect.

The only really striking decumbent brooms are both hybrids, Cytisus Beanii and C. kewensis. Cytisus Beanii is a hybrid between the aforementioned C. Ardoinii and the much taller C. purgans, and is partly prostrate and larger in all its parts than C. Ardoinii. I got it, grafted on laburnum, and for several years it flourished and cascaded down the steep dry slope. If I were growing it in a smaller place, I would get it from cuttings if I could, for I find own-root brooms best here, and I would place it where it would get more water. Cytisus kewensis, a hybrid of C. Ardoinii and C. multiflorus, is a far finer and more exciting plant. In the Pacific Northwest it can be draped over a rock wall and will hang down several feet, a lovely long lace curtain of creamy white. In California it is less vigorous and shorter in growth, but still, whether falling over our dry slope or leaning languorously over a low wall, it is mighty appealing in early spring.

MEDIUM HIGH BROOMS

In the list of brooms of medium height, say two to five feet, I give first place on all accounts to Cytisus praecox, an early one as its name indicates. It is a hybrid of C. purgans, presumably from pollen of C. multiflorus, and is nice and compact, a cherished characteristic where the family runs to ranginess. In March here it is always covered with small creamy flowers, a little heavy in odor; for the rest of the year it is clean and green and inconspicuous. I got a white-flowered form several years ago, I suppose a seedling, and it is clearer in color and a good substitute, where neatness is desired, for its lanky father, C. multiflorus. Unlike the cream form, it seeds and self-sows in our garden. Cytisus purgans one rarely sees, I don't know why, as it is a singularly attractive plant, the best of the medium yellow brooms; its small clear-colored blossoms give a very pleasant effect of light and cleanness without any of the casual character of many of the family.

Two of the medium-height brooms which have left us without too great mourning are Cytisus purpureus and its hybrid, C. versicolor, both of which I imported from British Columbia because I then wanted brooms in any color but yellow. They both proved to be shrubs about two feet high, undistinguished except in the purple color of the former and the purple, white, and yellow, the "versified" color, of the latter. They were never robust and eventually died out. Genista tinctoria, the last of the mediums, is one of the several summer-flowering yellow species valued chiefly for relatively late bloom. If you want one in midsummer, I recommend this, which is very easy, bright in color, and likely to perpetuate itself by seed; it grows here literally like a weed.

65

TALLER BROOMS

Of the taller brooms Genista monosperma is first early, its rigid, almost leafless stems reaching about ten feet, its rather small but attractive white flowers carried on short lateral racemes. Coming from North Africa and Spain, it is the most susceptible to frost of the whole family; I have lost it a couple of times. In warmer gardens it is quite worth growing for its slender lacy effect in early spring. As part of the planting of the dry slope between our house and the road and considered mainly as an inexpensive and informal screen, we grow that easy member of the family, Cytisus canariensis (Genista canariensis), mixed in with a few C. racemosus (G. racemosa), a much inferior species. C. canariensis is the florists' genista of eastern American greenhouses, but here it is perfectly hardy outdoors and its children spring up by the thousands from self-sown seed. It is highly drought-resistant and has no cultural demands. It is almost hidden in bright yellow flowers on short racemes in spring.

A Moroccan species, Cytisus Battandieri, probably because it was so highly recommended by David Fairchild, the plant explorer, was very appreciatively received as a seedling from a friend years ago. Its relatively large, soft green, silvery surfaced leaves were appealing. Some gardeners may care to cut it back hard occasionally just to get its pleasant foliage effect, but grown naturally here it shot up to about twelve feet, justifying the expectation of something more than its small yellow racemes of disappointing flowers. This spring we dispensed with it. A far better-known broom, one very widely planted a few years ago, Spartium junceum, we tried on our cool eastward-facing slope, but it apparently missed the heat and sun-

shine of former gardens facing west, where it did well. It is a
fine shrub, covered with fragrant flowers all summer, where
it is happy, but it seemed better to give its place here to more
contented things. One of these is Genista aethnensis, which is
admittedly rather tall, lean, and thin as to foliage, but perfectly
lovely when in flower in July, a season when few good shrubs
are in bloom. If you want a wide lace curtain of little yellow
flowers, plant it with a background so it will face your way,
preferably with a shrubby foreground to mask its long legs.
It is so generally admired each summer in our garden that it
is hard to understand why one sees it so little.

THE SCOTCH BROOMS

Cytisus scoparius is the tough and easily grown Scotch broom
of clear yellow. Though lovely in color, it has not endeared
itself in areas to which it is suited, for it has self-sown and become a nuisance in many places. There is a variety called C.
Andreanus where the wings of the pealike flower are dark red;
it varies a good deal from seed. Its greatest importance was as
one parent of the modern colored brooms. The other parent,
Cytisus multiflorus (formerly called C. albus), is what we call
here the Portugal broom, easily identified by its later tall leggy
growth and myriads of little white flowers in April. We planted
a number on a dry bank facing our house, and they were very
nice while young. They are rather short-lived, perhaps fortunately, for they can be replaced occasionally by young plants;
indeed they do it themselves here, and some of our unstudied
pictures have resulted from their springing up in unexpected
places. From C. scoparius var. Andreanus as seed parent and
C. multiflorus as pollen parent, a hybrid was raised at Kew
Gardens in 1900 and named C. Dallimorei. From the seed

produced by this hybrid and its progeny have come, with one exception, all the lovely variations now seen in nurseries and gardens from central California north.

HYBRID BROOMS

From English garden papers I learned of the existence of these hybrids, but nowhere could I find them in American nurseries, and it was too obviously love's labor lost to try to import, bare-root as United States Quarantine required, plants which disliked being moved even with soil on the roots and were always grown and sold in pots. However, English friends collected seed from named varieties in their own gardens and sent it to me in the fall of 1930. We sowed it at once in flats where it germinated a bit slowly and irregularly, but in all we got several hundred plants to set out in early spring where they were to grow. There they flowered, some in two, some in three years. As imported named varieties were not available, Victor Reiter propagated the best selections, which he later distributed. They were named for our colleges, California (pink), Stanford (mainly red), Pomona (orange and apricot), San Francisco (red), and St. Mary (white). Pomona proved the most popular variety, perhaps because it was easily propagated and its color is good, but it is rather tall, up to six feet. Personally I prefer the restrained medium growth, about three feet maximum, of California, from seed of which many pleasant pinks can easily be raised. For the raising of these brooms I received much undeserved credit; the only thing needed in getting them was persistence. The only skill involved was in their propagation. They come fairly well from cuttings of the ripened current season's growth taken from August on, and with the help of Rootone the percentage of success increases notably.

Later I was able to get from Vancouver, B. C., pot-grown plants of named varieties such as the tall red and cream Lord Lambourne and the fine red Dorothy Walpole. Anyone can raise from seed about as good varieties as those named if he will exercise care in selection, so I feel no urge to give further lists of names. There is, however, one pink broom, raised in England by crossing Dorothy Walpole by Cytisus multiflorus, and this more graceful and earlier hybrid, Geoffrey Skipwith, would be my first choice of all. Though I have collected seed from it, thus far it has failed to germinate, which is regrettable as the second shot of pollen of the Portugal broom naturally suggested that a whole series of smaller-flowered slender forms in varying colors might be obtained. Last summer I saw in Vancouver a lovely small-flowered broom which from its graceful growth may be of this parentage. It is called Johnson's Crimson, and after flowering it here this spring I am sure that it is the brightest and best of them all, a really lovely shrub.

The colored brooms can be very effectively used for garden decoration where they do well, as they bring brightness into the spring garden, but they have not done well in southern California and are perhaps not worth growing in warm and dry sections. They particularly enjoy summer watering, and it is probable that they do better in partial shade than in full sunshine in any but very foggy gardens. They are not long-lived plants, and though by light pruning immediately after flowering and keeping seed pods off, they can be kept thrifty for years, they lack the permanence of many shrubs. However, if they are well grown they give a lot for the money, which is pretty generous for brooms that are half Scotch!

CHAPTER SIX

AZALEAS AND CAMELLIAS

 FEEL fortunate to be living in California during the renascence of azalea and camellia growing. In climates favorable to their culture, as is much of California, they are among our most important shrubs and never deserved the neglect of the past—in the main a period of poorer taste in gardening. Where gardens should look clean and green the year around and where most of us are perhaps more interested in winter and spring color than in what we can get in our dry summers, they are doubtless due for increased popularity. Both plants have certain endearing characteristics. In a world where there has been too much pushing around, too much desire to spread without regard to one's neighbors, too much talk of places in the sun, it is cheering to be able to have plants which are not always pushing less assertive neighbors aside or growing over them, and are quite satisfied, even happier with only partial sun, and even enjoying considerable shade.

AZALEAS

Azaleas, botanically members of the rhododendron family, are quite capable, in cool coastal gardens with adequate facilities for summer watering, of becoming features as fine as those in the famous gardens of the old South. As the azaleas now most commonly grown are garden hybrids in constant process of variation and improvement, they are lovely and interesting as individuals as well as in masses. They can be used in beds and borders, along paths—particularly where there is some shade— against east-facing or other cool walls or house foundations, and of course they can be prominently planted with the main flowering season from March to May and with a good showing of late fall bloom on many of the evergreen kinds. Azaleas are fine for pots or redwood boxes on cool patios. We have found them happiest and most effective on the margin of a lawn, which is regularly watered by spray, and below a retaining wall facing east and opposite the front door, where they can be easily enjoyed.

Taken altogether azaleas are best adapted to eastern and northern exposures, with partial, preferably morning sun, though the deciduous varieties will stand a good deal of sunshine if they get enough water. They are of varying hardiness here, but even the relatively tender Indicas have come through our coldest winters with little or no damage, when we have had about a dozen degrees of frost. They have soil preferences, object to alkaline or lime soils, and are unhappy in heavy clays or adobes, but in neutral or preferably acid soils they thrive. They will grow well in almost pure peat, and a large amount of it should be incorporated in the soil for them, but our more vigorous varieties have certainly gone beyond the places we originally prepared for them, yet they are still doing well. Leaf mold and rotted pine needles are both good mixed in the soil or used as mulches. Where alkaline water must be used, dusting sulphur or aluminum sulphate should occasionally be sprinkled on the surface of the soil and worked in to keep it acid. Cottonseed meal, very lightly raked in after flowering and again in early autumn, will provide all the fertilizer they need. They must have summer water regularly, how often depending on season, exposure, and drainage; and overhead spraying is best. They need no cultivation, in fact it is detrimental, as the roots are so near the surface; weeding must be by hand. Azaleas can be moved readily with a ball of soil or peat at almost any time. Indeed for the highest culture, and particularly if plants are grown in pots, moving is desirable from time to time to make it possible to replace the peat, but this is quite unnecessary, we have found, for average success or general effect. Azaleas are all easily kept in shape by a little pruning or pinching back after they flower, but we find the deciduous species never need it and the others quite seldom.

TYPES OF PLANTS

Most amateurs will buy their plants, which in California are generally on their own roots, though some Indicas and named Ghents are grafted. On grafted plants one has to watch that the stock below the graft does not break out and starve the plant. More azaleas are now being supplied from rooted cuttings which are made from two-inch or three-inch pieces of unbloomed ripened growth of the current season, taken in late summer or early autumn—the lower leaves removed and the cuttings put about half their depth in a box or bed of sand, or of sand and peat—and started under glass. Cuttings take a month or more to make roots and must be kept moist at all times. The easiest way for the amateur to get a few additional plants of some preferred variety is by layering, that is, bending a low branch down so that a part of it can be put an inch or so underground and then surrounded by sandy, peaty soil. If the section of branch to be buried is slightly cut or scarified, or even if this is not done, a good many azaleas will form roots, and in a year they may be severed from the parent plant and set out by themselves. Named varieties do not come true from seed, but unselected azaleas can be raised in large numbers from fall- or winter-sown seed under glass. It is too exacting a job for most amateurs, takes too long to give flowering plants, and naturally produces many inferior forms.

Most of the azaleas grown in gardens are hybrids and can be separated into classes or groups, though future breeding may break down some of the present divisions. The deciduous azaleas—much hardier than the evergreen ones, though somewhat less adapted to California and more suited to the Pacific Northwest—are beautifully grown and wonderfully effective in gardens in Berkeley and in Marin County. The mollis hybrids, on the whole unnamed seedlings, are the most generally available of the deciduous series. They blossom before their leaves with heads of large flowers, mainly salmon reds, but including also buff, yellow, pink, and orange, all blending beautifully and at their best here in April. With them bloom the Kaempferi hybrids—taller with smaller flowers, mainly luscious pinks—which I find less adapted to our conditions and apt to burn in our warm spring sunshine. A little later the lovely maize-yellow Azalea altaclarense, one of the easiest doers, opens out, and it is followed by the Ghent and other deciduous hybrids developed by European specialists from eastern American and Asiatic species, and from our own deciduous A. occidentalis which sometimes bears rather small flowers but in a pleasing range of color, some coming with the leaves. Few of these fine forms are yet available here, but some amateurs are importing named varieties, and others are raising deciduous hybrids from seed. Two deciduous species may well be included in our azalea gardens, A. Schlippenbachii, a lovely pale pink from Asia, and our California native, A. occidentalis, which is usually white with a yellow blotch but occasionally comes pink. Foliage of most of the deciduous azaleas turns a beautiful red in late summer before it drops.

EVERGREEN AZALEAS

Evergreen azaleas, nearly all of them hybrids, are more widely grown here, and with justification, as they are better adapted to California conditions, and in addition to constant presentable foliage they offer great variation of habit and of flower.

The earliest of these, the Kurume azaleas from Japan, not hybrids but selections, have small foliage and relatively small flowers, single or double, and are generally dwarf compact plants giving a solid sheet of bloom when they flower in March or April. Hinodigeri, the brilliant crimson, is the best known. Of quite different origin is a newer series, the Rutherfordianas, much taller and rangier, but also with small leaves and flowers. These are probably not widely distributed yet, though I have grown them for several years and they have done very well. The Indica series, complex hybrids, mainly raised in Belgium and widely grown as pot plants under glass, have larger foliage, larger flowers, either single or double, and a wonderful range of color from white to red, with many variegated ones. The principal Indicas offered in California are fairly compact growers, unlike the older forms in the gardens of the old South. Among good doubles, which are the most popular type, are the pink and white Albert and Elizabeth, the pink Simon Mardner, and the white Vervaeneana alba. More of these fine hybrids are needed. Flowering with them here are several forms of A. ledifolia (A. mucronatum). These are much hardier and taller—up to six feet—and very vigorous and easy, layering freely, with grayer and rather hairy foliage and with the freest, most floriferous habit of any. We have immense bushes of the pure white (sometimes called A. indica alba), a lovely large white with rose patches on each petal (presumably Sekidera), and one or two rosy lilac forms. From importations of the United States Department of Agriculture we have secured a lovely series of the late Japanese A. macrantha hybrids—a fine single pink, rose and red selfs, and many odd variegated forms—which will be valued when they are more available, as they extend the season into June.

CAMELLIAS

Camellias have developed great popularity in California in the last decade and are now being widely planted both for garden decoration and for corsages. Though this interest is statewide, it is particularly noticeable in southern California, evidence that the camellia can stand more heat and drought than the more exacting azalea. Everywhere gardeners are recognizing that a good new camellia is an investment for a lifetime, that it grows slowly but produces more flowers each year, and that eventually it becomes an asset to the garden and the gardener.

Camellias require very little care. Though most of us prefer to plant them in half shade where they need less water and the flowers last long, they will grow in full sun, even if not quite as happy or effective there. Though they prefer an acid soil, they will accept a neutral one, and if young plants are properly planted in holes filled with well-mixed soil and peat, eventually, as the plants grow, their roots will work out into the ordinary soil of the garden. Young plants or those recently moved will need regular watering; we have found that a very occasional summer soaking is enough, but when the buds form, if rain doesn't come, moisture should be provided to prevent their dropping. Camellias are naturally slow growers, never lush or weedy, so they do not demand rich feeding. A handful of cottonseed meal, raked in lightly around each plant after flowering and again in fall, is all the fertilizing they need. Pruning is hardly ever necessary unless large leggy plants need it to reshape them. Cutting flowers with only two or three leaves, and letting the balance of the stem remain for new growth, is in itself pruning enough. But if topped, bushes will break out well again, as we learned last year when deer got into the garden and had an expensive meal off some of our plants.

Camellias are sometimes propagated by grafting, much more generally by cuttings. These should be about five inches long and of the current season's ripened growth. The best time to take them is in August or early September. Cut below a node, remove the lower leaves, shorten the others, and insert in a sand and peat mixture to a depth of about half the length of the cutting. If possible, place under glass. Camellias are slow to root so that amateurs generally prefer to save time by buying young plants, but the method is useful to know in case a cutting may be available from a friend and a rooted plant of the desired variety is perhaps hard to get.

Nearly all camellias are forms of Camellia japonica, but they vary greatly in form. There are singles, semidoubles, formals, rose-flowered and peony-flowered types in white, many shades of pink and rose, and red, and also in many variations of color. The nomenclature is badly confused, and the same varieties are sold by different dealers under many names. If you buy

76

from catalogs, it is better to select one good grower and get all your camellias from him, or actually to see from flowering specimens just what is being offered under a particular name.

SELECTED VARIETIES

It would be difficult to find a poor camellia. The following are certainly good ones, giving a wide variety of form and color and, what is quite important, a succession of flowers from late fall through winter till late spring: white—Otome White, Albaplena or Alba Fimbriata, Lotus (Grandiflora Alba); pink—Pink Perfection, Grandiflora Rosea, Marchioness of Exeter, Pink Ball (very pale), Debutante, Ecstasy, Kumasaka; red—Red Daikagura, Col. Firey, Elene Nobile (Napa Red), Flame; variegated—Hikari Gengi (Hermes or Jordan's Pride), Chandleri Elegans.

To start the season earlier, it is advisable to grow a few of the Sasanqua varieties, less erect, best against a support, and mostly with small single flowers. When you can afford it, add also the magnificent species, Camellia reticulata, with its huge ruffled rose-pink flowers on a widely branching, less compact plant than most camellias, still expensive, more tender than the forms of C. japonica, and a pearl of great price—but it will come down.

When a youngster in eastern Canada, I read in my big sister's Victorian novels how the hero (always of the privileged classes) proposed to the heroine in the conservatory and put a white camellia in her hair, little did I think that some day I would grow big bushes of camellias which would be perfectly hardy outdoors in California, with far more flowers on a single bush than would have provided King Solomon with corsages for all his fiancées—or wives.

CHAPTER SEVEN

PERENNIALS IN GENERAL

RITING of hardy perennials for California and considering them for climates of cold snowy winters and warm summers with frequent rains are quite different matters. In my earlier years in Montreal, perennials were the mainstay of most gardens. This was true everywhere north of Virginia and over the Middle West, and especially in places where winter snow was heavy enough to blanket the plants and keep out excessive cold. Where frosts came late in spring and early in autumn, annuals had short seasons; in very bad winters, uncovered shrubs were frozen back. Therefore the hardy perennials seemed best adapted to conditions. Being underground in winter but pushing up early in the spring, they gave some early bloom, extending in variety through the summer, and lasting longer into fall than the flowers of all other plants. The perennials in my Montreal garden enjoyed the period of complete winter rest and the warmth and rain of summer, and many of them grew with an abandon rarely seen here in California; their colors were better and the flowers less burned in the moist air of their blooming seasons. Their adaptability seemed almost perfect. True, there were drawbacks; some years, when the snow left early and alternate freezes and thaws occurred, there would be heaving out and winter killing, and sometimes excessive summer heat or heavy downpours of rain might catch the irises or the larkspurs, let us say, in full flower and cut the length of bloom in a wearying way.

When, therefore, I came here with the erroneous idea of most easterners that everything grew better in California, I had much to learn about perennials and their place in gardens. My changed ideas are due to gardening in a climate which has been described as having only two seasons, late spring and early autumn, a climate of a long cool, but not cold, wet "winter," and on the coast often a cool dry summer. I learned that perennials like the bearded irises, which come from the comparable climate of the Mediterranean, enjoyed California very much, but that many others whose forebears, like the herbaceous peonies, come from Siberia, or the phlox of the eastern United States, missed the long winter rest, snow blankets, summer rains, and moister atmosphere. Two great differences were also noticeable: first, the lengthening of the flowering time of many perennials, with—as you can't have it both ways—a less luxuriant period of full bloom; second, a garden year of twelve months instead of the more usual six.

This long season poses not only a personal problem for the gardener, who needs a rest as much as many of his plants, but also affects the growing and the use of perennials. Some, because they get inadequate rest, don't do as well here—eastern wild flowers, high alpines, and those from far northern climates are examples; others keep on blooming, leading a short life but a merry one, and then die young, as for instance, delphiniums and penstemons. But there are other results. Because of the absence of intense cold, plants rarely winterkill, although some are occasionally lost and more are weakened by lack of summer water. There are also a greater number of herbaceous perennials which are entirely hardy here, not relatively so, like chrysanthemums, penstemons, and red-hot pokers. These plants which are wholly tender in the east, the common geraniums and pelargoniums among them, are generally as permanent here as most perennials. Moreover there are many plants, such as snapdragons, petunias, verbenas, and others, raised annually from seeds and in colder climates always treated as annuals, which in California may be considered as biennials or short-lived perennials.

HERBACEOUS BORDERS

In modern gardening in England and America the popular place for growing hardy herbaceous plants has been the perennial border. Much ink has been used by writers to describe how this may be effectively done, with great attention to variety and proper placement of materials and to the making of telling color combinations by the association of groups which blend or contrast well. Last of all, writers explain how such a border, by a careful selection of plants, may be maintained at a fairly high pitch throughout the garden year, meaning of course the five months of the east, not the twelve of the west. Even to maintain a herbaceous border throughout what amounts to less than half our California garden year so taxes the ingenuity of eastern gardeners that perfectionists have been driven to making spring, summer, and autumn borders, to which in their particular seasons visitors will be directed in turn.

In California a hardy herbaceous border, in full enough flower for twelve months to make continual apologies unnecessary, is an unattainable objective. In Berkeley I observed for some years a most valiant effort to do this in a well-propor-

tioned double border set off by itself. Though well-tried
and undeniably attractive at its best, it confirmed my own
experience that the mixed border, only predominantly of
perennials, should be our substitute. Perhaps I am an in-
sensitive soul, but I have never been able to understand
why shrubs, perennials, bulbs, and annuals, even succulents
along the path, could not be expected to live together in
peace and beauty. In California at least tolerance is forced on
them.

In such a mixed border—perhaps the word combination
would be a happier term—careful consideration should be given
to location, to adequate sun, and to aspect, so that certain one-
sided flowers will face the path; then to deep digging and
thorough preparing of the soil, so that the border will serve
adequately for some years. The area planned may be for either
a single or double border; if single, it is best along a boundary
line; if double, on both sides of a wide path with some garden
feature, perhaps an arbor or arch, or maybe just a wide bench
across the end. If this area is drawn to scale on that squared
paper engineers use, a pleasant time may be had of an evening
or on a rainy day planning the selection of materials and their
arrangement. In general the tall plants will be placed in the
rear, and it is there that flowering shrubs may be incorporated
into the picture as a screen and for background, as well as for
their color contribution when in flower. Too rampant subjects
had better be avoided and so had straight planting lines, except in the rear ranks.

PLANTS FOR THE CENTER

The middle of the mixed border can be largely of perennials,
tall ones like delphiniums, kniphofias, and perennial sun-

flowers toward the back, with those of medium height, in the main, placed in front of them—irises, Japanese anemones, phlox, penstemons, and columbines, for example. However, the border will look better if it is not evenly sloped from front to rear, but broken into a pleasing variety of form by the occasional forward planting of taller material. Variety of contour may also be obtained by having regard for a suitable proportion of spires to rounded masses—larkspurs, lupins, montbretias being examples of perennials with spikes, and chrysanthemums, phlox, and geums of mounds. Accent plants are desirable to blend the whole, while the repetition of groups of the same thing also helps; clumps of tall bearded irises set at regular intervals will suggest what I mean.

EDGING MATERIAL

For the front, along the path, use the easier, stronger, and showier plants of the rock garden—aubrietias, arabis, alyssum, violas, or shrublets like the sun roses. Color harmonies and contrasts may be studied and tried; but with enough variety of material and color there will always be pleasant though unplanned combinations. Spaces through the border should be left for groups of the flowering bulbs of spring and summer—daffodils, tulips, the smaller gladiolus, and dahlias—and for the easier annuals.

Petunias or snapdragons of one color, planted over spring bulbs, will give a mass effect not obtainable by the use of restless mixtures. In such a border, even on a small place, great variety of material may be grown without achieving the formality of a botanical garden or seed farm. It is in these mixed plantings that the hardy herbaceous perennial will make its greatest contribution to the garden. Of course separate plantings of preferred perennials like irises or chrysanthemums may still be made and grown in such variety as to become a specialty of the garden.

METHODS OF INCREASE

A few suggestions may as well be given now regarding the cultivation and the development of stock with which to furnish borders, though more specific instructions will also sometimes accompany the comments on individual perennials. Some perennials can be satisfactorily increased only by propagation from an existing plant, by divisions, or by root or stem cuttings. Irises, phlox, and peonies come in this group because plant-breeding specialists have raised many thousands of these from seed—generally the results of cross fertilization—and those named forms offered in catalogs are selections from their best seedlings, the rest having been discarded. The specialists' offerings are furthermore the survivors of many varieties which have been introduced, and most of them will be superseded as improvements are effected. Such garden or horticultural varieties, as they are called, do not reproduce themselves true from seed, but any part of the parent plant which can be used for vegetative propagation will give exactly the same kind of offspring.

Propagation by division is generally a simple process, better done for most plants in California in autumn at the time of the early rains, when the separated segments, each with some roots, can be replanted at once. But many fall-flowering perennials, chrysanthemums, perennial asters, and sunflowers among them, break apart more easily when the new growth comes up in early spring. Where there are a number of old clumps, they may be rather roughly pulled apart and the new growths replanted, as in the case of irises, but if stock is scarce or valuable, it is better to wash all soil away from the roots and carefully divide the plants to single crowns or pieces, using a handfork or a knife to assist if root stocks are tough. No special care is necessary afterward, but early replanting and watering are helpful in re-establishment; in any case do not weaken the plants by leaving them around for the air to dry out their roots; if they can't be replanted soon, dig a trench, lay the plants along the sloping side with the roots below and the tops on the surface, and fill in with soft soil to keep the divisions in good condition.

Propagation by root cuttings—a common commercial practice for Japanese anemones, phlox, and oriental poppies—greatly increases the number of smaller plants procurable from one clump or from one large plant, but is a more particular operation. Fill flats with good potting soil, lift the parent phlox or anemone, shake off all dirt, and with a sharp knife cut all the roots into pieces an inch or so in length. Spread these pieces over the flat and cover with soil so that they are about a quarter inch beneath it. In the case of oriental poppies it is better to cut the parsniplike roots into sections a couple of inches long and insert these, top up and about two inches apart, in a somewhat deeper box. In due time, root sections make top growth, and when it is evident they are well developed, perhaps in three months or so, they can be dug up and separately potted so that they can make good root systems before being planted out to face a hard world.

Some plants are readily increased by cuttings of the stem; geraniums, penstemons, chrysanthemums, and gazanias are examples. Propagation by stem cuttings is not a difficult process, but as the cuttings start without any roots, they need considerable care in watering, shading, and protection from drying winds until they are rooted. A cold frame, or for a small number of cuttings a bell glass or even a wide-mouthed bottle, is of great assistance. The best general growing medium is sand, but often a combination of sand and fine peat is used, as many cuttings root best in such acid conditions. In recent years commercial aids to rooting, either liquid or in powder form like Rootone, have greatly increased the facility of rooting plants and the proportion of takes.

Only experience can teach a gardener how to handle difficult plants, but certain general rules may be accepted: (1) cuttings should be taken from the tops of new stocky growth, not from flowered or spindly stems; (2) cuttings may be from one to three inches in length; (3) they should be cut clean across just below a node or point of leaf growth; (4) the lower leaves should be removed from that part of the stem which is to go beneath the soil; (5) the remaining leaves should be cut in half to reduce evaporation. Shading and frequent sprinklings are necessary for some time until it is evident that the cuttings will not flag without such attention. When new growth starts it is easy, by lifting cuttings from underneath, to see if they have enough roots to justify potting up in regular soil or setting out in prepared beds for growing until they are strong enough to be planted in their permanent places. Most propagation of perennials by cuttings is done in spring when new growth is available.

GROWING FROM SEED

Hardy perennials can also be raised from seed. This is not worth doing if superior named varieties are offered, nor is it profitable to spend the time and give the care to raising seedlings when the purchase of a plant or two will soon provide clumps which can be divided into many sections. Yet in some cases it is by far the cheapest way to get a lot of material. Specific forms, that is, unimproved wild plants, come true to seed and so are suitable for raising in that way. The hardy alyssums and candytufts, the different species of flax, anthemis, and campanula, species of dianthus, lathyrus, lychnis, lupin, and primula are but a few of those worth raising from seed. It may take a little time, but from seed you can grow plants as good as you can buy, and your stock will be young and vigorous. Perhaps more important, however, is the fun, the adventure.

Seed from garden forms of popular perennials has been so developed by breeding or selection that it will give a large proportion of fine forms or a wide range of lovely colors. From seed you will have not only the excitement of watching the first flowering of the plants you have raised, but if you buy really fine, sometimes rather expensive seed, you will get strains superior to those which general nurserymen can afford to supply in plants. You may even be able to select some outstanding individuals from which you can propagate vegetatively or give to friends. A few perennials worth growing from seed are the long-spurred columbines, polyanthus primroses, delphiniums, penstemons, pyrethrums, perennial scabious and gaillardias, and wallflowers. Without doubt, vigorous young plants, moved right from seed bed to garden, will also establish themselves better than plants which have been dug up, packed, shipped, inspected, and delivered for planting only when time allows you to attend to them.

Raising perennials from seed is not quite as easy as raising annuals. I doubt if satisfactory results can ever be counted on in California from open-ground sowing right in the garden. The hazards of cold or drying winds, blistering sunshine, and drenching rains are too great. A small greenhouse or lath house is desirable if you do a lot of sowing, but good results can be obtained, as I know from much experience, if a seed bed or seed frame, provided with a glass sash or a lath screen, is used. In California this is best placed in half shade. The soil should be light, a mixture of garden loam, rotted cow manure, and sand, with pulverized peat substituted for humus, if it is more readily obtainable. Avoid adobes or heavy clays for seed starting. August is perhaps as good a time as any to sow, since the fresh seed crops of such perennials as primroses and delphiniums are available by then, but about this there can be no rule for every plant and every gardener.

Some perennials flower the following year from midsummer sowing, but others take longer. Germination is slower and more irregular than with annuals, often a month compared with a week for annuals, and until the little plants come up, the seed bed must be kept shaded and moist but not wet. As germination occurs, lessen the shade or the seedlings may get spindly. When they have made considerable growth, and have developed at least one pair of true leaves, they should either be thinned out or, if you want all the plants, they should be carefully transplanted to stand two or three inches apart in prepared beds of good light soil. Here they should be given more sunshine and grown on until, their nursery phase being over, they are strong enough to be put into the permanent places where they must face the competition of their neighbors amid the dangers of communal life.

Perhaps it is easier for the gardener to sow seeds in flats, the three-inch depth of which is enough for most plants while they are young. A simple platform at table level in partial shade will hold the flats enabling one to work at an easier height than on the ground. The use of flats also permits greater variety of soil mixtures and treatments, including earlier removal of those perennials which germinate and grow quickly. Such flats should have adequate drainage and be filled with prepared soils. The surface of the soil should be leveled with a block, and the seeds scattered thinly and covered to a depth of about four times their size. In most cases just covering them from sight is adequate. Watering too can be more conveniently done for flats, with fine sprinkling for little seeds and heavier watering for larger ones, and after germination occurs for seedlings. I also prefer to prick out the little seedlings into other flats, planting them an inch or two apart. After they have become well established, they may be hardened off by moving the flats into a more open location. Of course if this seed raising is done in a greenhouse or a lath house, flats will be used to conserve space and facilitate moving out.

CONSIDER THE SOIL

Suggestions for border culture will frequently be given in the notes which follow about specific plants. Here it is enough to say that preparation of the soil for long-time herbaceous borders is generally inadequate. The English dig the soil a couple of feet deep; in America we rarely go more than one. Deep digging affords an easier root run and conserves moisture where it is needed; it is, I think, more important in most gardens than fertilizers. I realize that I do not feed my plants enough, and if it were readily available, I would like to supply more humus through the incorporation of that rare material, good old cow manure, but the feeding of particular flowers or the enriching of patches can be continued after planting and throughout the life of the border by forking in commercial fertilizers, while, later, deep digging is difficult if not impossible.

CHAPTER EIGHT

PERENNIALS IN PARTICULAR

J HAVE chosen to comment on particular perennials alphabetically. This at least facilitates finding them, but not all the perennials will be found here. Some of the smaller ones are discussed in the chapter on rock plants; others, like dahlias, under Summer-flowering Bulbs; still others, like irises or geraniums, in special chapters. From my years as a librarian I urge readers to use the index.

ACANTHUS

Our list begins with acanthus, on a note of gloom. My attitude toward it was unfavorably fixed when in my early years a schoolteacher, regardless of the fact that my artistic bent did not turn in the direction of the graphic arts, insisted that I produce a drawing of the acanthus leaf, which she said the Greeks had conventionalized and used decoratively in their architecture. Little did I think then that in California I would get personally acquainted with Acanthus mollis, the plant which was the source of my early trouble. Naturally I decided here to master it. I found it really a very distinct and decorative plant, and one almost too well adapted to California, where it is perfectly hardy. Its great glossy green leaves are distinct and beautiful, and though its three-foot flower spikes bear curiously shaped flowers of rather dull rose and white, even they have a certain architectural value in early summer. I hoped to remove my early frustration by proving I could grow these leaves even if I couldn't draw them, and I succeeded only too well.

This acanthus, once planted in either sun or shade, increases by underground growth, and new crowns appear in our garden at long distances from the original planting; sporadic digging and poisoning have not eradicated them from where they were unwanted. With this warning, I recommend the planting of acanthus in the wilder parts of gardens where their habit of dying down in summer will not leave a bare or unsightly place and where their complete indifference to summer drought will be an asset.

ACHILLEA

Achilleas or yarrows, some of them tough citizens with the bad habit of encroaching on their neighbors, give us some fair rock plants and one or two pretty good border subjects. Achillea ptarmica (A. salicifolia), the sneezewort, of which there are several garden forms, the best known being The Pearl, is of some value in cold climates for the white flowers it gives on two-foot stems for cutting, but with its wandering habit I doubt if it is worth a place in California gardens. The slightly shorter A. millefolium (the common milfoil), with flat heads of odd shades of rose—I remember it in the old-fashioned covering of my grandmother's sofa—is easy, drought-resistant, and more restrained; there is also a dark rose form, but none is very important, though they do give variety. The species I have found really desirable is A. filipendulina (A. Eupatorium), with sparse fernlike foliage and stems up to four or five feet, each ending in a flat head of bright yellow flowers which last for weeks, fading finally to old gold. Not only is it a good cut flower even when old and dry, but its flat flowers are valuable in the rear of the border as a contrast to such spirelike perennials as the delphiniums; it is also easy and drought-resistant, and will do well for a long time without division. All achilleas can be increased by division of the roots at almost any time.

ACONITUM AND ALYSSUM

Aconitums or monkshoods seem better suited to gardens in the eastern half of our continent. A correspondent sent me a nice set of several varieties, but they resented the dry conditions of our hillside and never amounted to anything. This must be common experience, for I find them rarely if ever offered in catalogs, though one California grower lists Sparks' Variety, an improved form with dark blue flowers, recommending a cool moist situation and fall in preference to spring planting.

Alyssum saxatile is so robust and easy a perennial that it belongs to the front of the herbaceous border even more than to the rock garden, its decumbent habit and gray foliage patterning the hard edges of paths and giving them a pleasant variation of leaf color throughout the year, for in California it never loses its foliage. Far into spring it is covered with little racemes of such a rich yellow that it is often called Basket of Gold. There are also more compact and double forms, but to me Alyssum saxatile var. citrinum, or Silver Queen—though this last seems a misnomer—is the best for most gardens, its pale yellow associating far better with other colors than the harsh bright yellow of some forms. I find alyssums easy, quite drought-resistant throughout our long summers, and prone to self-sow and provide me with additional plants. As these have rather woody stems they do not divide readily and are in any case best left undisturbed for years. They root from stem cuttings, but raising them from seed is easier and plants so obtained are better.

ANCHUSA

Of anchusas my experience is limited to the best known, which Bailey now calls Anchusa azurea but which is still A. italica in nursery catalogs. Its tall stems, up to five feet, break out above rough hairy foliage into sprays of flowers of forget-me-not form and of a beautiful clear blue, especially in improved garden varieties. In cold wet climates this importation from the Mediterranean occasionally winterkills. In California it appears to be permanent, almost imperishable in fact; though in one case I dug up all its woody roots to a depth of a foot, it came up again right through a gravel path. Yet it is not to be classed as a nuisance, and it is useful for its color and long spring to summer season of bloom for the rear of borders or in rough places. Any division of the tough woody root will grow, so propagation by division is easiest, but this anchusa also comes from seed.

JAPANESE ANEMONES

Japanese anemones, garden forms of Anemone japonica, are highly desirable and are here particularly adapted to cool eastern exposures. As anemones are often caught by early frosts, breeders sought for colder climates earlier flowering varieties like September Charm, which is unimportant for California, where older forms generally flower in August, although we would like to have them later. There are several nice single varieties, ranging in color from pure white to deep pink or purplish rose, but perhaps because they resemble the common cosmos too much or because they last less long, I would give first choice to such semidoubles as the white Whirl-wind, to Queen Charlotte, the best shade of light pink, and to Prince Henry, a dark, almost red variety.

When planting these anemones, make up your mind where they will look and do best, perhaps in a northeast angle of the house or some semishady place in the border where they will get regular summer watering until after flowering. Set the plants a foot or so apart, for they will spread and eventually mat together, and then leave them there for years. They need a year before much bloom can be expected, but after that period of waiting they can be relied on for a pleasant show of graceful windflowers, on stems two or three feet high. Increase anemones by divisions or offsets which have stooled out, or by root cuttings if a great many little plants are needed, not by seed, which is slow and would give inferior single forms. The flowers are not much good for cutting so leave them for garden decoration.

ANTHEMIS

Anthemis tinctoria, sometimes called the hardy golden Marguerite, is the most commonly grown of a family of herbaceous plants with feathery pinnate foliage of distinctive odor. It is a relative of the dwarf carpeting plant, A. nobilis, from which camomile tea is made. However, it is A. tinctoria which is valuable in the border for its ease of culture, resistance to drought, and long season of pleasant yellow daisies on stems about two feet high. It does want a sunny place, and its flowers stay open longer there, but it is one of those perennials which stand neglect and may be left long undisturbed, though it responds well to occasional replanting. Propagation is from seed or by division of the roots. This and another species, A. Sancti-

Johannis, are good material for the middle of the border, the latter being less vigorous here, but of such a fine deep orange color that it also should be grown.

AQUILEGIA OR COLUMBINE

Aquilegias or columbines are lovely and distinctive perennials, having fine foliage and a lightness and grace in their flowers which make them a garden asset either alone or distributed through a border to tone down more assertive things. Except in rock gardens, wild forms or species are now less grown, gardeners properly preferring the improved forms—with wider petals, larger flowers, longer spurs, and more colors— which years of selection and crossbreeding have produced.

My first experience was with the rather dull, dumpy, but culturally complacent forms of the common European species, A. vulgaris, characterized by the absence of long spurs. They are easy in California; there is a nice pure white form in our garden still, neglected but persistent. It is hard to find a superior strain of A. vulgaris because breeders have been restricting themselves to improving the lighter, more graceful long-spurred columbines. These were bred mainly from certain western species—the very lovely but here rather temperamental pale blue and white A. coerulea, from the colder and wetter conditions of the Rocky Mountains, and the yellow A. chrysantha and the red and yellow A. Skinneri, both from warmer and drier locations and therefore naturally happy here. The average gardener either will buy plants from nurseries which, let us hope, have grown them from the better strains, or he will raise them from seed. In my experience large plants divide very badly and suffer too much from shock; they do not even like being moved when old.

So it is best to start with young seedling plants, very easy to do, as the tiny seeds germinate well if started either in autumn or early spring and kept cool and damp for three or four weeks. The seedlings are easy to grow on until they can be planted in their permanent location, which should be in one of the cooler, shadier places in the garden. Many strains of long-spurred hybrids are offered, all of course as the best. I have found that the widest selection of nice clear colors, with desirable size and width of petals, are found in the more expensive mixtures sent out by Waller Franklin, by Suttons, and by Dobbies (whose strain is grown, I think, by Ferry-Morse in America). Self-sown or casually collected seed tends to deteriorate; selection of seed from only the best flowers is essential.

ARABIS AND ARMERIA

Among the rock cresses, Arabis albida, though it may clothe large areas in rock gardens, is rather rampant and so is better fitted for the margin or path planting of a border. The single type with its grayish persistent leafage and little spikes of white flowers is pleasing and can be readily raised from seed or increased from cuttings, but I now grow only a double form—too rarely found—with little stems suggesting miniature white stocks. This double form lasts much longer but can only be increased by cuttings.

Armerias, commonly called thrifts, have provided me with one nice border plant utterly unlike the little Armeria maritima of path edgings and primitive rockeries. From a cushion of foliage, which dies down considerably in times of summer drought, wiry eighteen-inch stems rise in late spring, each topped by a pink ball of florets of a really good color. I cannot identify it, but it is probably Sutton's Giant Pink, similar to Wayside Gardens' Tall Hybrids, in white, rose, and pink shades, but none is quite as good as mine, which has had some distribution from seed handouts.

ASTERS

Perennial asters, notably Aster novae-angliae and A. novi-belgii, are common wild flowers of late summer and autumn, particularly on the eastern side of this continent. In nature they are weedy and their starlike clusters of blue or of red purple are not too bright. But as with many other American plants, their improvement was undertaken by English specialists, and from their finishing schools, these asters returned to us as named varieties of what the English have always called Michaelmas daisies. Fired by pictures of their use in English gardens, I bought many varieties, including all the recently imported novelties. From this experience I can only commend their culti-vation to those whose time and garden conditions allow them to grow these modern asters really well; they require culture similar to that of chrysanthemums. Gardeners with hot dry places had better leave them alone, but in small level gardens, where they can get summer attention, they will do much to carry the herbaceous border through late summer, which is their season here, with its height in August rather than in fall around Michaelmas Day.

The named varieties represent careful selection. One should therefore find a modern collection in a nursery or catalog, buy one of each reasonably distinct variety, and later discard any that are inferior or too much alike. The plants stool out and increase to an incredible degree. At the Panama-Pacific Ex-position in San Francisco in 1915—now it can be told—I celebrated the closing day by snitching a single rooted stem of the fine lavender Climax. If from the plant which subsequently developed I had divided and replanted each piece every year for five years, I am sure I could have covered the county with it.

Asters are gross feeders, and for really good results the clumps should be dug up each spring and the young outside single growths with good roots separated and replanted in groups to make nice clumps. Such annual digging with fertilizing of the ground and replanting—all pleasant exercise in a small garden—mean too much work in a large one. But under good culture these asters are very rewarding with their certain clouds of misty blue, pink, white, or purple just when our gardens are getting bare, except for annuals. As they are continually being improved, any list of recommended varieties would be dated. There is also a delightful race of dwarfs of comparable culture which make cushions of color and, in my garden, flower freely, some at six inches, others growing up to twelve. They come from England with such names as Countess of Dudley (pink), Victor (lavender blue), and Noble (white); they really have a place in small summer gardens. So has the hybrid—of different parentage from most of our garden forms— Aster Frikartii, a plant about two feet high, with lavender flowers, two inches across, and a restrained growth which keeps it within bounds and does not involve annual replanting. I commend A. Frikartii without reservation.

ASTILBES

Astilbes—often listed as aruncus or herbaceous spireas—are pleasing plants of bushy form, the cut foliage forming a base from which grow stems carrying lovely plumy heads of white, pink, rose, or red. They are widely grown in pots by florists and

98

PORTFOLIO

OF

PICTURES

TAKEN IN THE

AUTHOR'S GARDEN

BY

ALMA LAVENSON

1. *Azaleas and a Fountain of Broom*. Forms of ledifolia and indica below a low stone wall, with white Portugal broom leaning over the shrub-covered bank.

2. *Gracious Entrance.* The front door facing the terrace is enlivened by the early and very fragrant flowering shrub, Osmanthus Delavayi, growing next the Chinese pottery.

3. *Camellia Sentinels.* Entrance to the living room from the patio with a pair of matched Camellia Kumasaka in flower.

4. *Veil of Cherry Bloom*. Japanese cherry Mikuruma Gaeshi (Mitchell's single pink) faced with a broad planting of deciduous azaleas along the path north of the house.

5. *Narcissus Slope.* The north end of the double border of daffodils running across the garden far below the house, with a
background of Prunus Mume Dawn and two forms of Magnolia
Soulangeana.

6. *Hyacinth Simplicity*. An informal planting under apple trees gives a Dresden china effect. Behind the hyacinths, Scilla campanulata Excelsior blooms later.

7. *Brilliance with Iris*. Tall bearded seedlings, selected and raised by the author, are being tried out as individuals and groups in a large bed near the house.

8. *Native Beauty*. California native irises, forms of I. Douglasiana, cover the steep slope below the terrace and demand no care and no summer water.

9. *Loveliness on a Wall.* Phlox camlaensis, best of the creeping phloxes, is massed over a low wall where steppingstone paths meet.

10. *Foamy Accent.* The lovely creamy white Cytisus kewensis on the steps to the patio. In wetter climates it grows much longer than this fairly compact specimen.

11. *Magnolia Drama*. Lennei, the latest of the deciduous hybrids, has stunning flowers of heavy texture, white inside, a rich glowing purple outside.

forced into bloom under glass; under their essential conditions they are also excellent in the open border. Intrigued by their beauty in gardens in the Puget Sound country, I acquired a set of fine forms, but failed completely with them here. Perhaps in small level gardens where they can be kept constantly moist in summer they may be worth growing in California, but their insistence on conditions not natural here is discouraging to the average gardener.

CAMPANULA

Most of the campanulas or bellflowers which I have grown have been rock plants and will be discussed elsewhere, but there are in this large family, among a good many mediocre and some pretty bad species—Campanula Grossekii for example has proved to be an almost ineradicable weed here—a few perennials really worth having. My first choice would be C. lactiflora (syn. C. celtidifolia), a tidy plant for the mixed border. From a cushion of fairly large toothed leaves, C. lactiflora throws up in midsummer three-foot stems with large heads of fine blue flowers as big as those of a perennial phlox and of a color too rarely found in summer flowers. It is best raised from seed and left alone where it is happy. The other good border species is C. persicifolia, the peach-leaved bellflower, which is more generally grown. It makes mats of long narrow foliage and from each crown in late spring and through early summer come spikes about two feet high, with blue or white bell-shaped flowers clustered around the upper half. There are larger grandiflora forms and a named variety, Telham Beauty, which is just about the best. All these can be raised from seed (though the named one doesn't come true), or any form can be quickly increased by dividing to single crowns, preferably in autumn or early spring. The campanulas have no special cultural demands, but seem to do better if divided and replanted every few years.

CHEIRANTHUS OR WALLFLOWERS

Cheiranthus Cheiri may mean little to us gardeners, but it is the name botanists have given to that valuable short-lived perennial commonly called the wallflower, a word which should suggest no social derogation but merely that it often grows in retaining walls in Europe. In a world willing to pay much for synthetic scent it is regrettable that certain plants like the wallflowers with attractive natural perfume should be so overlooked. Their chief need is a cool growing and flowering season—winter or early spring in California—conditions which can be given readily in many of our gardens, particularly those around San Francisco Bay. In England or British Columbia, wallflowers are more often used for bedding or as a ground planting for tulips than as hardy perennials.

Wallflowers are available in yellows, bronzes, browns, reds, even odd shades of pink, and the florets on the spikes, which resemble single stocks, come out together and last a long time. They are best raised from seed, which is rarely available in this country in any but mixed colors, although English seedsmen offer separate color selections. Seed should be sown in flats in early summer, and the plants set out by early autumn in the places where they are to bloom. In bedding they are discarded after flowering, but in the border they can be left for another year or two as they are short-lived perennials; in such a situation their later, taller growth—they should not be cut to the ground—may be a bit untidy, but they will look the more natural for it. The Siberian wallflower, Cheiranthus Allioni, now called Erysimum asperum by Bailey (but I retain the older horticultural name), is really a North American wild-flower, even a native of California mountains. It is less formal in habit, with later, lighter stems of wonderful orange flowers, easily raised from early fall sowings, which produce blooms the next spring and thereafter, though this wallflower also needs frequent renewal. The narrow gray-leaved Cheiranthus lini-folius (Erysimum linifolium) is a lower one-foot plant with smaller pleasant lilac flowers; it calls for the same treatment. I grew these minor species at one time and liked them both.

CHRYSANTHEMUMS

Chrysanthemums, that is, the plants commonly so designated by florists, are treated as a specialty in a later chapter. At this point, however, attention should be given to certain members of the family. One, a hardier, tougher one than the garden chrysanthemum is Chrysanthemum maximum, often called the Shasta daisy, its big yellow-centered white-petaled flowers having been developed into such huge singles as Alaska or Mayfield Giant, such doubles as Esther Reed or Mt. Shasta, and such daintier fringed variations as Chiffon. As there are already fine selected forms which would not come true from seed, it is wise to start with plants of these in spring. After a year each plant will have spread into a clump which can be left a second or third year by indifferent or busy gardeners. It is much better, however, to dig them up early each spring and to split them into smaller pieces and replant in well-dug and fertilized soil.

Chrysanthemum frutescens, the Paris daisy or Marguerite, in California generally develops into a shrub, often huge in size. As it is readily renewed by cuttings, it can be kept within the bounds of a border plant, and is useful for cutting, being a persistent bloomer. Specimen plants can be kept shapely by pruning, to which they submit without sulking. One dwarfer species I must mention is C. Mawii, a little half shrubby pink and white perennial from Morocco, which I grew from seed. It is a short-lived plant, not showy but nice for variety, and enjoys sunshine and a dry place.

CONVALLARIA OR LILY-OF-THE-VALLEY

Easterners who miss lily-of-the-valley in California gardens frequently ask if we can grow this plant, which carries the rather weighty botanical name of Convallaria majalis. The answer is that academic irritant—yes and no. It is yes if you can provide a suitable site, a cool shady place; suitable soil, that is, one which is cool, moist, and enriched with plenty of old leaf mold; and last, suitable stock, which would not be composed of old crowded clumps but of good strong pips or single crowns, such as are grown for forcing. If you plant these fairly close together in the fall, you can certainly expect flowers the following spring, but whether you can get them regularly thereafter depends on meeting their requirements. The answer is no if you are counting on the ease and success you may have had in the east, where old shady beds of lily-of-the-valley spread in all directions, even as I saw them in my sister's garden in Winnipeg last summer, where the plants run under fences, undeterred even by concrete divisional copings. In California their permanence is doubtfully attainable.

COREOPSIS

The perennial Coreopsis grandiflora (C. lanceolata var. grandiflora) is the best of the family, a native of our Southwest. It never winterkills here, in fact with me it self-sows and, if out of place, has often to be pulled up like a weed. Its large yellow flowers, coming singly on tall stems, are bright in the border and good for cutting, but it goes to seed rather quickly and so should be used more sparingly than where seasons are shorter; it is also rather short-lived. I think some of the annuals of the family really give more for the money and effort. We have also several native California species which are perennial, C. Douglasii, C. maritima, and C. gigantea—all of them formerly separately classed as Leptosyne—but these are a bit weedy and straggly for gardens.

DELPHINIUM

Delphiniums are among the most important hardy plants, invaluable for the rear of the border, where in rows or clumps their tall spires of pure blues as well as many shades of lavender, mauve, purple, and more recently white add height and accent and a pleasing variation to what might otherwise be too flat an effect. They have undergone such remarkable development in the last years that they have now become a specialty with many gardeners who, understandably, prefer to grow them separately, both for their massed magnificence and because in that way the plants can be given preferential treatment to obtain the grand spikes of large flowers possible from the modern race. As compared with the old delphiniums of my early gardening days, today's varieties may have lost something of ruggedness, of permanence, and of propriety for blending with other things in a general border, but if now, like fine ladies, they need extra care, they repay it with their individuality and with a glamour their ancestors lacked.

In England and to a lesser extent in the eastern United States, named varieties—propagated by division or by cuttings, the latter not an easy process—have been distributed, but I believe that in California, with our different growing conditions, plants raised from seed rather than from divisions are to be favored for their garden vigor; I suspect, too, that permanence here is not as possible as in places where the plants can rest half of every year in frozen or snow-covered ground.

For seed we formerly depended on English growers, and the Wrexham and the Blackmore and Langdon strains had many adherents. The one which has had greatest national acclaim, the Pacific strain, happens to have been developed in California by Frank Reinelt, one of my best friends, so that over the last dozen years I have visited his plantings annually and observed the great advances made in the several color classifications. He is fully persuaded that improvements will continue to be so rapid that it is inadvisable to select particular plants for naming and vegetative propagation, as they would be too rapidly superseded by their seed-raised descendants. I am sure that this has been true so far, and that in California at least plants raised from seed will continue to be preferred. There is the additional argument that here, in the nature of things, a good many delphiniums are short-lived perennials, wearing themselves out. Moreover, as they are so readily raised, it is worth while pursuing a plan of constant renewal, inasmuch as the best individual spikes come on young plants. Whatever the strain of seed, there is good reason for either getting it from the originator or in his original packets, for while some general seed growers may be particular in selection, others simply buy stock seed of named strains for their own sowing and then compete in price but not in quality with the originator, failing to keep up the strain by careful and costly reselection.

Under California conditions growth from seed is so rapid

that delphiniums will produce their first flowers in a few months from sowing. If this is done in early spring, bloom can be expected the same autumn, while from seed sown about mid-summer a first flowering should occur the following spring. Sow seed in flats in a mixture of two-thirds coarse leaf mold and one-third loam, covering the seeds lightly. Shade the flats with paper or with paper and glass until germination occurs, generally in about two weeks. Then the covering should be removed at once, but the flats kept in shade and the soil constantly moist. Frank Reinelt writes that for best germination bottom heat is necessary, with a cool temperature overhead. In a greenhouse in early spring these conditions can be met, but in midsummer he recommends that where it is warm the flats be put on the floor of a cool shed and kept dark for the first ten days; a lath house is a good place to start delphiniums and many other seeds. When the true leaves have developed, the little plants should be pricked out—that is, transplanted from pans to flat boxes—to stand about three inches apart and then hardened off to full sunlight before being set out in the garden. Select places in full sunlight and avoid the proximity of walls or drafty locations which are hospitable to mildew. Soil should be well dug and fertilized, and water regularly supplied during the growing season.

In California a second crop of spikes can be expected. Mr. Reinelt advises cutting off all spikes of the first crop just above the foliage and giving the plants a rest for two or three weeks; then, when new growths appear, cut the old stems to the ground, sprinkle some ammonium phosphate around each plant, rake it in lightly and water well. As the new shoots will usually be too numerous, if fine spikes are wanted, retain a very few and remove the others. He believes that forcing the plants to make more than two crops of flowers a year reduces their vitality to the point where many of them perish. If mildew appears on the foliage, immediate sulphur dusting is helpful, but it is almost useless if plants are already badly affected. Good breeders are continually trying to eradicate susceptibility by selection of mildew-resistant seed bearers for their stock. Crown rot is not the problem in California it sometimes is in the east, but our western growers, especially along the coast, have to contend with a virus disease called Green Flower; as there is no cure and it is spread by leaf hoppers, all affected plants should at once be destroyed.

Attention has been so concentrated on the giant hybrids that the usefulness of other species and varieties of delphiniums for inclusion in mixed borders is often overlooked. There are a number of more slender looser-growing forms with smaller much-branched stems, apparently from D. cheilanthum, which are classed as Belladonna varieties and are pleasant if less exciting plants. For the front of the border there is D. grandiflorum (more often listed as D. chinense), easily raised and quickly flowered from seed, and limited to deep blue, pale blue, and white. As these various delphiniums are dwarf, two feet or more high, and bushy, they have their own place. We have also several native species, of which two are most distinct in color. The scarlet larkspur, from southern California, is best raised from seed, as plants cannot be moved readily, except in cans. In full sun it makes tall much-branched wiry stems and has hardy mildew-free foliage. Less striking is the red larkspur, D. nudicaule—yellow forms are also found—slender, one to two feet high, and quite distinct. As D. nudicaule comes from the cooler coastal areas farther north, unlike D. cardinale, it will endure, indeed prefer, a semishaded location. From an accidental cross of it, apparently with a tall garden larkspur, came the salmon pink, listed in America as Sensation, which it certainly was. However, it had to be propagated by cuttings or divisions and seems to be dropping out of commerce. I have not grown or seen it in California, but in Vancouver, B. C., it appeared very happy and worth while. I would hardly hope for its permanence here, in spite of the acknowledged preference of even half Californians, like this plant Sensation, for their own state.

DIANTHUS

The Dianthus or pink family is particularly happy in California, and I am sure a larger number of its members can be grown successfully outdoors here than anywhere else in America. The double hardy garden pinks or border carnations of English gardens and the far finer, taller American carnations of greenhouse culture can be grown quite successfully outdoors in California, the former favoring the northern and the latter the southern end of the state. But the habits of carnations, which are not graceful or tolerant of neighbors, the necessity of staking and of disbudding, invalidate them as border subjects and indicate that they should be grown apart, as a specialty or for cut flowers, rather than for garden beauty. They like a well-drained soil in full sun, and young plants should be kept pinched back to develop many basal shoots. When a good plant has been grown, let the flowering stems develop, and as buds form reduce these in number to get large individual flowers on long stems for cutting.

For border use, and they can be very appropriately planted on path margins to break a rigid line, I would limit myself to good garden forms of the old cottage Pink, Dianthus plumarius, with single flowers of white, pink, rose, and red, frequently with darker centers, coming by the dozens in late spring from mats of low gray persistent foliage. Pick up fine varieties where you can, or even more interesting as I have found, raise a batch of plants from some good strain of seed. A greater variety of seed will be found in English catalogs. When the plants bloom, discard those least liked and, if any particular ones are preferred, increase them after the blooming period by making tip cuttings of the unflowered stems. They will root readily in sand if they are shaded and kept moist. These hardy pinks like sunny places and good drainage and prefer an alkaline, that is, a sweet or lime soil, rather than an acid or sour one; they are easy and long lasting but after a few years are best replaced by young plants.

DICENTRA

Dicentra formosa, a California native variously called Western Dutchman's breeches or pink bleeding heart, is a nice twelve-inch species from a family with fine fernlike foliage and distinct and pleasing flowers. These dicentras all like cool shaded woodsy places, such as fern gardens with moist soil. Dicentra spectabilis, the old bleeding heart of our mothers' gardens in the east—it is one of the first flowers I remember seeing growing as a child—is taller and a better garden flower. It is about two feet high, and its unusual rosy red, hanging heart-shaped flowers held well above the foliage are worth while for themselves even if they lack a sentimental appeal for you.

DICTAMNUS OR GAS PLANT

Another old plant which is less seen here but worth trying for variety is Dictamnus albus (D. Fraxinella), with the popular names of dittany, gas plant, and burning bush. It is a long-enduring perennial, doing best when well established and left alone. The common form has flowers of an odd shade of rosy purple though there is a white, less attractive variety. Its volatile oil gives it a not unpleasant odor, and its reputed characteristic of lighting to a match is responsible for its old names; it generally fails to perform, in my experience.

DIGITALIS AND DIPLACUS

The common foxglove, improved varieties of Digitalis purpurea, is more generally biennial than perennial, but in California it self-sows, even naturalizes, as evidenced along the coast north of Eureka. It is best raised from seed sown outdoors and grown in the rough, wild shaded places. Its value in perennial borders is limited; better grow it by itself, somewhere out of the way on the north or east side, so planted that the flowers will face the sun and the path.

Diplacus, native to California, is certainly a possible border plant. Bailey includes it under the wholly herbaceous mimulus or monkey-flowers, but it seems better to retain the name diplacus. In various species it extends from San Diego into northern California and even to the northern Sierras, bordering our mountain roads and flowering in late spring and early summer. The most common species are D. puniceus, generally red, and D. longiflorus, orange yellow, both in southern California; D. aurantiacus, orange yellow, in central and northern California; and D. leptanthus, in the northern Sierra Nevadas. Each of these species seems to do best in the gardens of the section where it is native, but to some extent special consideration to aspect will broaden possibilities. Natural hybrids or those raised in gardens have not only combined the good garden qualities of species but have given us larger flowers and a greatly widened range of colors, including white, cream, buff, orange, red, and some lovely pale apricot pinks. All may be raised from seed, best sown in early spring or late fall in flats, the seedlings potted up and set out when a few inches high. Well-grown they flower in a few months, the trumpet-shaped blossoms appearing profusely from the axils of the growing shoots and well above the foliage. In autumn when the plants look shabby, they can profitably be cut almost to the ground, and in spring they will send up fresh new growth very much in the manner of herbaceous perennials.

Fine selected forms of diplacus can be easily perpetuated by tip cuttings, best made in early spring from the new growth. D. aurantiacus and what appear to be hybrids have naturalized in shady places in our garden, and it is evident even here that they prefer some protection from full sun. After seeing glorious patches of D. leptanthus cascading down the northern slopes of the Feather River Canyon, like cream and buff azaleas in effect, I tried it here; but our place is rather dry for this high mountain species, which does better in the native garden of the Tilden Regional Park below us, where it gets more shade and water. Those further interested should read a fine paper by the director of the Santa Barbara Botanic Garden, Maunsell Van Rensselaer, "Diplacus for Gardens and Roadsides," published in the *Journal of the California Horticultural Society,* October, 1944.

DORONICUM AND ECHINOPS

Doronicums, old perennials of European gardens, are rarely seen in California; they are more prized in colder climates, where Doronicum caucasicum sends up its large graceful, single, daisylike yellow flowers sooner than almost anything else in the herbaceous border and provides cut flowers when there are few. I doubt if any other species is worth growing in California where we have so many more exciting daisies.

Echinops or globe thistles and eryngiums or sea hollies I have classed together because their striking gray-green much-cut foliage provides an unusual note for the border and their metallic blue flower heads attract particular attention there. These are effective as cut flowers, lasting long after quite dry. Echinops ritro is the only globe thistle commonly found in catalogs: it is a tall plant, up to three feet, with globular blue flower heads. More important are the eryngiums, of which I still grow Eryngium amethystinum, with its glistening bluish bracts in striking design. Nomenclature seems mixed, but this variety is about two feet high and flowers here in June or July. There are others like the taller E. planum, but one is enough. Eryngiums are easily grown and best left alone unless more plants are wanted, when they may be divided if they have not stooled out as they usually do here. Both echinops and eryngiums can also be raised from seed.

ERIGERON, FELICIA, FRANCOA

Erigerons are numerous, and a few are useful for their low growth, up to eighteen inches, and lavender, lilac, even orange daisylike flowers with finer petals than most composites. Erigeron The Quakeress did nicely for a time here but died out, probably from our failure to provide adequate summer moisture.

Felicia amelloides (Agathea coelestis), the blue daisy, like a number of other South Africans is quite happy here, but not able to stand really cold weather. It is a compact plant, about eighteen inches high, subshrubby for its foliage is evergreen, and the small blue flowers can be found all through the year; it is quite worth while for color and for its good habit and disposition. It can be raised from seed and increased by cuttings.

When I first found Francoa ramosa in California there ended a frustration started in the early years of gardening when I read about it in Gertrude Jekyll's *Colour in the Flower Garden*. On the Atlantic coast it would have been too tender for outdoor culture, but here this Chilean perennial is very much at home in gardens and invaluable because it loves shady places; though it enjoys summer watering, it thrives even when that is forgotten. From a foundation of pleasant persistent foliage, in midsummer and often scatteringly at other times, it throws up three-foot wandlike stems clothed with the white flowers which justify its English name of maiden's wreath. Francoa sonchifolia is similar but in pink shades. Both can be raised from seed, although this is probably unobtainable except from English seedsmen or from a Californian who grows them; they self-sow in the shadier, moister places here. Plants can be increased by division in fall or early spring, and I would not be surprised if cuttings of stocky growth would readily root. Francoas deserve wider use in California, particularly in cool coastal gardens. They ought also to be tried as pot plants, as Miss Jekyll used them, for semishaded patios.

FUNKIA OR PLANTAIN LILY

The plantain lilies, which I grew in the east as funkia (now botanically called hosta), are not very important in California in spite of their clumps of distinctive foliage, which rather than their spikes of white flowers give them garden value. I have not been moved to try them, but if I had a cool damp shady border where ferns did well I might again grow them, though I don't like that name plantain—it meant much weeding of lawns long ago. Hosta plantaginea (Funkia subcordata or F. grandiflora) is the species most commonly grown; it is hard to raise from seed but easily increased by division of crowns.

GAILLARDIA

The perennial gaillardias, sometimes called blanket flowers because of their predominantly yellow flowers with red bands, are tough natives of our northwest prairies and tablelands, yet they are almost indestructible in California, probably because they not only endure cold in their natural homes but also drought, which they get here. They are easily raised from seed, prefer a sunny place, and like good drainage. Though a bit plebeian, they are so continuously in flower and useful for cutting that they are to be found in many gardens. Their drawback is a somewhat lax or untidy habit, but particularly fine forms with more compact growth have been developed. These have to be increased by division, in spring or fall, or by cuttings made in late summer.

GAURA

Gaura Lindheimeri, from Texas, is tall, growing up to four feet. It is a perennial which Carl Purdy used to recommend to California gardeners. Its loose terminal spikes of small white flowers add a certain lightness, like lace, to borders of heavier things; it is also drought-resistant.

GAZANIA

Gazanias, South African perennials with foliage frequently evergreen in California, have been given the name of treasure flowers in England, which they seem to justify under our favorable conditions. Because they have little frost resistance and therefore were not grown in the older and colder parts of America, they were not brought to California by gardeners moving west. Only in recent years have their beauty and utility been recognized here. One species, generally referred to as Gazania aurantiaca, has long been used as a ground cover and is readily recognized in parkings or along paths by the almost blinding brilliance of its daisylike orange flowers, open only in full sunshine. Occasionally too a larger, taller yellow gazania is found in gardens, but only recently, from imported seeds, have Californians seen what variety of color and markings was possible. Now there are a few named forms like Victor Reiter's brilliant orange-red Fiesta, and Paul Howard of Los Angeles offers seed of California Flowerland Everblooming Padre Hybrids.

Given ordinary soil and full sun, for the flowers will not open without it, the plants throw up single flowers well above the foliage in a great burst of bloom in spring and more sparingly throughout most of the year. In our garden they grow in large clumps on a steep bank, along paths, and anywhere we let them, for they self-sow every winter and seedlings appear casually each spring. They now come in white, cream, yellow, orange, red, and even in a few pink and rose shades in selfs or stripes, and with a great variety of fascinating basal spots in delightful designs. The easiest way to get a start is from begged or bought seed, sown in flats in fall, the seedlings later moved into the garden; these seedling plants flower the following summer and for years thereafter. Because of the great variation of plants from seed, selected forms must be perpetuated by stem cuttings, if their foliage has stems, or by very careful division of the crowns, rootless pieces being treated as cuttings and put in a propagating box of sand. Character of growth naturally varies a good deal in what is now a hybrid race. Collecting, breeding, and selecting gazanias is a wide open field for any amateur. My best pink forms, nice compact growers, came from an Atherton amateur, Harold Johnson.

GERBERAS

Gerberas or Transvaal daisies are also South African perennials, hardy outdoors in California, but by reason of their habit of growth, their special cultural needs, and their effect of sparse rather than full-massed flowers, they are not very valuable as border plants. They are best grown in rows by themselves, as in the case of carnations, and in the main also for cut flowers, though they can make a nice bed by themselves when in full flower, the long narrow graceful petals coming in an unusual range of color from white through cream, yellow to orange, and from pale pastel pink to deep rose and crimson. There are now also double forms which, however, do not seem to do as well in northern California.

Gerberas can be raised from seed, but a friend who has much success with them says the seed must be fresh and preferably newly gathered; that the best soil mixture for the flats is half sand, a quarter loam, and a quarter coarse leaf mold or peat; and that as the seedlings must have good drainage, the pot, pan, or flat should be supplied with a bottom layer of gravel. Seed should not be covered over a quarter of an inch, and while soil should be kept damp, it must never get soggy. The young plants, pricked out into other flats or potted up, may be planted out when they have made from three to five true leaves. Easier of course is propagation by division of the crowns, each section being taken with a few good roots and leaves; these sections can be planted out at once in the garden. Crowded old clumps may either be lifted—you can rarely get all the deep roots—or sections may be cut out for division; this can be done at almost any time, but autumn is preferable.

Select a sunny place for gerberas. The character of the soil is less important than that it be well drained and not allowed to cover the crown or center of the plant. Water thoroughly by irrigation; not by frequent sprinkling. Gerberas will stand little winter cold and need protection even in some parts of California. Established clumps bloom well in spring and again in late summer, with occasional flowers appearing at any time in warm areas. Some growers advocate gently pulling the stems from the base to avoid accumulation of old growth. It has been found that splitting the stems of cut flowers an inch or so from the base lengthens the period they last, which is unusually long in any case.

GEUM

Geums provide both rock and border plants. For border use, the most satisfactory are the improved double forms of Geum chiloense (G. atrosanguineum), a robust Chile species with large persistent leaves and stems up to two feet, with several flowers in the shape of giant double buttercups. The red double, Mrs. Bradshaw, is good in itself but a shade, like some geraniums, which is hard to associate with others. Lady Stratheden, a double golden yellow, fits into a border planting better, but my first choice is Princess Juliana, with double orange flowers.

As the inflorescence is not heavy, it is wise for garden effect to plant geums in groups rather than singly. While they can be raised from seed, it is better to buy small plants of the named doubles. Any good garden soil in sun or half shade will suit them, but they enjoy quantities of water and require it for continuous flowering. If left unmoved for some years, they tend to get woody, and the foliage grows too high above the ground, so occasional division and replanting are desirable.

GYPSOPHILA OR BABYS-BREATH

The best known, in fact the only widely grown perennial gypsophila for the border is Gypsophila paniculata, the hardy, tough, deep-rooting drought-resistant, and long-lasting babys-breath, which in its single form has long been prized for the filmy cloud of little flowers which cover its two- to three-foot much-branched stems, a very useful flower to soften color combinations in the border or to cover the ripening foliage of spring bulbs. Now there is a fine double form, Bristol Fairy, which like all the doubles must be propagated by cuttings or grafts, and a double pink form of G. pacifica, named Flamingo. They are easy to grow, but their deep roots like to be let alone, so select for them a place where they may remain undisturbed.

HELENIUM

Certain members of the daisy family, all yellow or red, have been too little used in California gardens, partly because the better forms have not always been procurable. I have tried in California many heleniums, helianthus, and heliopsis in the past years, so I shall pass on my experiences. I prefer the heleniums even if they bear the ominous old name of sneeze-weeds, which in their case involves no responsibility for hay fever. They are perfectly hardy perennials, with crown foliage of long lanceolate leaves from which rise in midsummer and later—but not in autumn here as in colder climates—stiff erect stems from eighteen inches to five feet high according to variety, each topped by a flat head of many flowers, the centers like balls, with petals tending to drop a little below them. To get the best forms, plants must be bought, and fortunately more of these are available than when I got mine from Oregon and British Columbia nurseries. Heleniums thrive in a fairly rich soil and like a sunny situation and lots of water through the summer. They also appreciate occasional division of the clumps, for best results about every three years or so, in fall or early spring.

The varieties most commonly listed are forms of Helenium autumnale; Riverton Beauty, yellow with a brown center, and Riverton Gem, with petals of yellow and terracotta, finally turning to wallflower red; both plants for the rear of the border. I prefer, however, certain newer varieties of medium height, to about three feet, and earlier flowering; among them, Madame Canivet, a yellow with chocolate center, and Moerheim Beauty, a glowing solid red, still seem the best. The earliest and dwarfest is Pumilum magnificum, not over eighteen inches, with masses of golden yellow flowers. The big heads are most effective in the border and for cutting, and the plants show a commendable restraint in growth not shared by all their relatives, the perennial helianthus or sunflowers.

HELIANTHUS OR SUNFLOWERS

Sunflowers should be limited to the back of borders or to wild gardening. Some species are reasonably compact, like Helianthus mollis, H. atrorubens (better known as H. sparcifolius), to which the fine variety, Monarch, belongs, H. decapetalus (H. multiflorus), responsible for some rather mopheaded doubles for which I have little enthusiasm, and H. angustifolius, the narrow-leaved swamp sunflower, which with summer watering does very well with me and is about the best of the family for California, flowering late and very freely. While I knew that there were some perennial sunflowers which encroached on their neighbors, it needed a personal experience to teach me to leave H. rigidus and H. salicifolius (H. orgyalis) and some named varieties, like Miss Mellish, derived from them, alone. Why aren't we told more often in nursery catalogs or in garden books of the terrifying spread of which their stoloniferous roots are capable?

HELIOPSIS AND HELIOTROPE

Heliopsis, on the contrary, when we grew them, always kept themselves to themselves and proved good neighbors. They are tall but more compact and equally easy to grow, flowering in midsummer in California. The best for gardens are Heliopsis helianthoides var. Pitcheriana and H. scabra, with several named forms, including one, Incomparabilis, which received acclaim in England and sounds good, with its rich golden yellow flowers made up of several rows of petals.

In some warm places in California it would be quite legitimate to call the heliotrope of fragrant memory a hardy herbaceous perennial, as it rarely winterkills. Where, as in our garden, one gets occasional "unusual" years with several degrees of frost, it is better to plant it only in pots or in some warm protected corner of the house against a north wall, where it will face the sun. Better buy plants of selected forms and increase them by cuttings if more are wanted. It asks for an open sunny location where, unless cut back by frost, its foliage is persistent.

HELLEBORE OR CHRISTMAS ROSE

Only in recent years have I recognized the desirability of hellebores for our gardens in winter and their happiness in California, if they can be given shade and moisture. Now I heartily commend them to other gardeners for their clean varnished and almost evergreen palmate foliage and their dozens of two-inch single five-petaled flowers, which occur in white to purple, including green, and which large clumps here produce from Christmas to April, on about eighteen-inch stems. The flowers, which last for months, are undamaged by rains and slowly change in color. As cut flowers they attract attention for their novelty and their odd and what some might call decadent colors. The two species commonly grown are Helleborus niger, the Christmas rose, with solitary mainly white flowers, and H. orientalis, the Lenten rose, with several flowers on each stem and in the wider range of color already mentioned. We also were given and still grow a plant of H. lividus (H. corsicus), which is less effective but interesting for its pale green heads of flowers. It is still hard to find hellebores in California catalogs. Mine came originally from an old friend, Toichi Domoto, of Hayward, whose nursery has contributed much to our garden. Carl Purdy was the only grower I knew who listed named English hybrids. I believe that most hellebores grown in California are also hybrids, and you can afford to forget whether they are Christmas or Lenten roses as they all flower as soon as the cooler weather and the rains stimulate new growth. Our hellebores are planted on a bank which is watered all summer by sprinklers and is quite shady. A fern bed would be an equally desirable location. Ordinary garden soil will do, but if it is enriched by manure and lightened with sand, hellebores like it better. Self-sown seedlings come up all over our planting in winter, but they take about three years to flower. Better start with plants, which bloom best when left undisturbed for years. Do not expect immediate effects when you divide the clumps in autumn, though our experience shows we can move big unbroken ones then without loss of a season's bloom.

HEMEROCALLIS OR DAY LILY

Day lilies, species and hybrids of hemerocallis—this Greek name means beautiful by day, for in most forms the flowers close at night—are imperishable perennials, enduring great cold and quite considerable drought. In gardens in the older and colder half of this country, two species have long been grown. Hemerocallis flava, the sweet-scented lemon lily, which may still be found growing around the foundations of old houses, burned or abandoned many years ago, is desirable, but H. fulva, the tawny day lily, a larger, coarser species with rusty red flowers, so vigorous and long-living that it has escaped to roadsides east of the Missouri, seems to me less necessary for our gardens.

In the last two decades, day lilies in new named varieties have had greatly increased popularity due to the activities of plant breeders, particularly in America. A cult has arisen similar to that of the iris, but I question if the hemerocallis has the inherent characteristics which have been responsible for the wide popularity of the iris; limitation of color is the most evident drawback. Nevertheless, many wider open flowers in all shades of yellow from light canary to deep glowing orange, far deeper and clearer reds than those of the old H. fulva, browns and clouded or grayish pinks, and many variations of blending or throat markings have already been achieved. Quite as important, newer varieties have so extended the season that we may now have some varieties in bloom from spring to fall. All they ask for is good garden soil in sun or light shade. They flower from divisions quite soon, but are at their best when established and need only be lifted and divided into single crowns when they get crowded, in perhaps four or five years. They stand great heat and considerable drought, but they really like summer water and in fact are often most effectively planted around pools or ponds, where their somewhat tuberous roots are kept wet by seepage or overflow.

A number of years ago I bought what were then rated the best, among them Calypso, Hyperion, and Mikado, still good standard varieties, but I was disappointed that they lacked the abandon and luxuriance of growth and flower I expected from their reputation elsewhere. Recently a friend whose garden is in the hot plain north of Mt. Diablo told me that experience in California had shown that these day lilies want warm summer days and resent cold and fog at that season, naming gardens in Salinas and east of Los Angeles as places where they grew really well. So gardeners like myself who revel in cool summers must give up emphasis on a family which resents them. The largest California list of hemerocallis which I have seen is that of the Milliken Gardens in Arcadia, and the biggest eastern collection that of Fairmont Gardens, Lowell, Massachusetts. Specialization in them is not for me, but it may be for you.

HEUCHERA

Heucheras, alum roots, are western American perennials from rocky or mountainous places, several of them natives of California. They are most commonly grown in rock gardens, but they are also suitable for borders and, having nearly evergreen foliage of distinct and attractive character, they make good marginal plantings. Any well-drained soil in sun or shade seems to suit them. By far the best known is Heuchera sanguinea, coral bells, with light panicles of little flowers of the red color and the shape suggested by their popular name. Well-established plantings are effective in full flower all through the spring. When plants get old and woody or infested with mealy bug, their occasional pest, lift them, break up the clumps, and keep the newer growing sections. Dip them in a nicotine solution to destroy the mealy bug, if it is evident, and reset them a foot or so apart, where they may be left until they grow into close mats. I once had a very good hybrid, Rosamund, with taller stems and larger panicles of a paler coral pink. Our natives, H. micrantha, with filmy white flowers, and H. rubescens, with pinkish ones, are less showy than forms of H. sanguinea. There is still room for the raising of a finer race of heucheras by blending the good qualities of the better species.

HOLLYHOCK

Hollyhocks are garden forms of althaea, but are so much better known by their popular name that they are mentioned at this point. At one time Berkeley gardens, parkings, sometimes even vacant lots, were gay in June with their tall stems, furnished with big wide-open single flowers in many colors, most of them from self-sowing. Now they seem to have disappeared, perhaps discouraged by gardeners because of their untidy if picturesque habit, perhaps reduced by hollyhock rust. They are biennials, flowering the year following the sowing of seed in the same place where the plants are wanted to bloom. There are gorgeous double strains, but they look a bit formal for their way of life, and the plants seem less vigorous.

KNIPHOFIA OR TRITOMA

Kniphofia is now the difficult but preferred name for what were once botanically tritomas, and are commonly called torch-lilies or red-hot poker-plants. They are far better perennials in California than in climates where they are often winterkilled. At one time I was much interested in the family, collecting them where I could and even raising them from seed, an easy though slow process. It is better, however, to pick the best garden forms and divide them when more are wanted. They make great clumps, some with evergreen foliage, and as it is quite a job to move the bigger ones, it is fortunate they continue to flower for years without division. Though it is chiefly the tall ones which are seen, there are miniature species for farther front in the border and also races of medium height. Of the giants, I still grow the variety I bought as H. F. Dreer (probably really Kniphofia uvaria var. nobilis, an English hybrid), at its best here in June, with great spikes of orange scarlet, and a variety which closely follows it, raised by Luther Burbank and called Towers of Gold, a name descriptive of its growth and color.

I also like and grow a glowing red hybrid of medium size and August flowering called Pfitzeri. From the late Major Vanderbilt I received years ago a dozen varieties of a race he had raised, all of medium height, with grassy foliage and more slender spikes of white, cream, yellow, apricot, orange, and red, which were early, floriferous, and better adapted to cutting. Similar named hybrids or proprietary strains are now offered by plantsmen. The kniphofias are appropriate for planting around pools or ponds or in wild places, as well as for accents in borders or as clumps for striking effects.

LINUM AND LOBELIA

In the selection of linums or flaxes for California gardens the element of hardiness does not need to be considered, so it is best to forget species like Linum perenne (L. sibiricum) and grow the far superior blue flax L. narbonnense, from the comparable climate of southern France. This you can get easily from seed or from offsets around the spreading plants, which otherwise may be left undisturbed. Give full sun as the flowers do not open in shade, and don't worry much about watering as it is very drought-resistant. The other perennial flax we grow is the white L. monogynum, from New Zealand, also about two feet high and of the same easy culture. Neither of these ever dies to the ground here.

With Lobelia cardinalis I have had no success here, for like so many eastern American natives used to acid soil and summer moisture in the ground and atmosphere, the cardinal flower seems sickly here. As I desire a garden, not a sanatorium, I limit myself to what is healthy under our conditions. Perhaps Californians with different conditions, a continually damper soil for one, may be able to grow it well enough to make it worth while; I cannot.

LUPINES

Our inability to grow the hardy herbaceous lupines, so wonderful in color, so floriferous and effective in English gardens, is another matter, for it is a great deprivation that we cannot have them in California. These are selections due to breeding within the species Lupinus polyphyllus, a native of the Pacific coast from northern California to Washington, flowering in June, obviously thriving in the road ditches and in flat wet meadows, never growing on dry hillsides. The essentials of ground water, moisture in the air, and absence of summer drought limit the use of the beautiful garden varieties to climates like those of the Pacific northwest and of the British Isles. It is the English who have specialized in these lupines, and from their fine seed selections and named varieties are obtainable all colors from white through pink to red and from pale blue to purple, with many lovely bicolors and blends in tall full spikes of pea-shaped flowers.

When the special selection known as the Russell hybrids was sent out and widely publicized, many good California gardeners tried them; some grew and exhibited them. With special attention to location and watering and by a constant struggle a measure of success is possible in our cooler coastal gardens, but I am pretty sure the average gardener will not fight long to give them the home conditions we lack. Better leave them to north Pacific gardeners, but if you must have them, either get a good English strain of seed, which will produce flowers the year following sowing, or buy plants from Oregon or Washington nurseries, and do not blame anyone if they don't match the pictures.

Our hope is that by breeding and selecting other native perennial lupines, from warmer, drier places and of drought-resistant nature, we may develop a race worth growing here. I had hoped that the rather shrubby tree lupine of our sandy coasts, L. arboreus, might be easier. It varies a good deal in color, as instance the plantings along U.S. Highway 101 just north of Eureka, but L. arboreus requires a very sandy soil indeed and failed as badly for me in our heavy loam as did its strictly herbaceous relative. Perhaps its variety L. Paynei, from further inland, may be the best with which to experiment. In the meanwhile we can content ourselves with annual lupines, of which we have some choice.

LYCHNIS

In the east I grew with some satisfaction, because they were easy, hardy, and colorful, certain species of lychnis, Lychnis calcedonica, three feet high with flat heads of vivid, really scarlet flowers; L. Haageana, one foot, with flowers variously called scarlet and crimson; and L. viscaria, the double form, sometimes called ragged robin, and described as rose crimson, a euphemism for magenta. I gave them up here as we have better perennials for our conditions, and their violent colors fight with their neighbors unless the latter are carefully selected for peaceful purposes.

MEGASIA OR SAXIFRAGE

I shall use the name Megasia crassifolia for what was once called Saxifraga crassifolia and which Bailey now carefully conceals as Bergenia crassifolia. It is utterly unlike the saxifrages of rock gardening, a husky perennial with large evergreen leaves turning somewhat reddish in winter, when the plants send up eighteen-inch stems with panicles of cold rather purplish rose flowers which last for a long time when other garden flowers are scarce. It is a good perennial for cool parkings, to edge semi-shaded beds facing east, or to plant with ferns. It is never untidy, but being a little off-color, it is best appreciated for its season when it does not have to face much competition.

MORAEA AND MYOSOTIS

Since I am particularly addicted to the iris family, it is not surprising that I grow some of the related moraeas from South

Africa. The commonest in California is certainly Moraea iridoides (Dietes iridoides), with evergreen two-foot sword-like leaves and considerably taller, almost permanent flower stems, which should not be cut down because along them from time to time appear very pleasing white irislike flowers with yellow basal blotches. An odd feature is the way the intermittent flowers, usually through summer, occur on all plants at the same time without respect to their location. It has recently been claimed that they follow certain phases of the moon. Big established plants producing many of the evanescent flowers are worth having. Leave the plants alone, though they transplant well and divide easily for increase at any time. Moraea bicolor, with lemon-yellow flowers spotted brown, is less grown and really less desirable, but might be included for variety. No particular culture is required, but give all moraeas a sunny situation.

Forget-me-nots, botanically myosotis, may be treated in California as annuals, biennials, or perennials. They come so readily from seed it is unnecessary to buy plants, and injunctions to protect them in winter may be disregarded. They deserve growing because their little blue flowers are desirable and cover the ground nicely in shaded places kept from getting too dry. Seed sown even in the open ground, in late summer, flowers freely the following spring and if conditions are good, the old plants will persist and self-sow.

NEPETA

Nepeta, a family of mostly aromatic shrubs, including Nepeta Cataria, catnip or catmint, includes one, N. Mussinii, which like most plants from the Caucasus and Persia does well here, is perfectly hardy, and makes a fine edging or front plant in borders, its aromatic grayish foliage being attractive even without the many spikes of clear lavender flowers above it in late spring. After flowering is past, the foliage gets shabby, but if cut back, nice new clean growth comes up, sometimes with a minor flowering.

Get plants of the species or of one of the newer named varieties—not very important improvements on it—and put them in well-drained sunny places for they are decidedly drought-resistant. When they get crowded or matted, they can be broken up and replanted, after blooming or in fall, or if you prefer to start again with young vigorous plants, you can root these in great numbers by putting cuttings in a sandbox. Take pieces a couple of inches long of the new young growth which comes up after cutting back in early summer. Some gardeners tell me that their cats ruin even N. Mussinii by rolling on it in ecstasy, but our cat never does so, though sometimes after a too hearty meal of quail, not on toast, he will eat young pieces of the foliage, perhaps for the same purpose as weaker humans resort to sodium bicarbonate—he can't tell me!

NIEREMBERGIA

Of the nierembergias I have grown and can recommend as a pleasant but not very striking plant, Nierembergia frutescens, a three-foot rather shrubby species, a native of Chile, with white saucer-shaped flowers tinted lilac. From Argentina another dwarfer, showier species, properly N. caerulea—though it was distributed as N. hippomania—came a few years ago. Its deeper lavender-blue flowers with yellow eyes were attractive, but it has proved to be so short-lived a perennial and so quick to flower from seed that it is commonly treated as an annual.

PEONY

The herbaceous Paeonia albiflora, parent of the beautiful and often sweet-scented hardy herbaceous peonies, comes from Siberia. Its descendants still naturally prefer cold winters and, quite as much, moisture at the roots all summer, conditions difficult even to approximate in most California gardens, but more nearly possible in the foothills of the northern Sierras or on the floors of the cooler coastal valleys.

I grew peonies in eastern Canada. Then after twenty years of enforced abstention here, I saw a fine collection in bloom in June in Seattle, got the desire for them again, and the following fall planted about fifty in the most favorable place in this then new garden, a swale with deep rich soil, our coldest place in winter and warmest and wettest in summer. The soil was dug in September to a depth of about two feet, and the nice large divisions from northern nurseries were planted some three feet apart, with the dormant but then very evident eyes within two inches of the surface, not deeper. The plants were well watered in, and after a couple of flowerless seasons when they were getting established, and during the summers of which they were several times irrigated, they began to bloom. For years they have given us fine cut flowers in late May and June, though I cannot say they have ever been as lush or as effective garden plants as they generally prove to be in more suitable climates.

Addicts who resent being without peonies here and who can give them deep rich soil, perhaps some summer shade, and certainly water during our dry season, have a measure of success. I know of commercial growers in the Santa Clara Valley and have in my files a peony list from San Jose. But if your garden is on a dry sunny slope, or in summerless San Francisco or winterless southern California, it will be best to pass peonies by. Of course a possible alternative is to grow only tree peonies, forms of P. moutan, which give perfectly stunning flowers and are on the whole better adapted to our climate, but they bloom in spring and are by no means easy in most gardens; besides the shrubby plants are rather ugly except when in flower.

POPPIES

The perennial members of the large papaver or poppy family differ considerably from each other. Unquestionably the two most important ones everywhere, even in California, where climatic conditions greatly affect their culture, are Papaver nudicaule, the Iceland poppy, and P. orientale, the oriental poppy.

Iceland poppies, when I first grew them in Montreal, were short-lived perennials, mounds of gray-green lobed leaves from which in early spring grew twelve-inch wiry stems, with yellow or, rarely, deep orange or white flowers, sweet-scented and good for cutting, for which purpose they are best cut in bud. Through the efforts of plant breeders, stronger strains have been developed with taller stems and much larger flowers and in a wider range of most delicate colors, cream, buff, pink, apricot, salmon, and coral red, as well as the original ones. In California these poppies are short-lived, not because they winterkill as they did back east, but because they dislike our long dry, sometimes warm summers. Treat them as biennials, sowing the seed in early autumn in flats or seed beds under lath, with only a sprinkling of sand over them. Unlike most poppies, they transplant readily and can be pricked out about two inches apart before final planting out or if conditions are very favorable, they can go directly into their flowering places. Give them sun, and if they get their preferred sandy soil, they will do better than in heavier ones. In fertilizers, avoid those with much nitrogen. Plants spaced six inches to a foot apart will make nice beds or border patches. Early autumn sowings will give flowers in spring when moisture conditions are best for them and chewing insects have not yet appeared to deface the flowers. After flowering, it is better to discard the plants and start another lot later. There are a number of excellent strains of seed. As I happen to like the newer colors, I have particularly enjoyed the Australian Gartref and Gartford strains.

If the oriental poppies are seen less in California than in other American gardens, it is not because of insufficient appreciation of their beauty but due to relatively less success in achieving that perfection possible in colder and wetter climates. This failure is surprising as their parents came from areas east of the Mediterranean to Persia, but possibly their habitat is colder in winter or wetter in summer than ours. My observation has been that the greatest measure of success is possible with plants well etablished in partial shade, where their deep parsniplike roots get plenty of moisture just before and during flowering; it seems to matter less thereafter as they have a rest period after blooming. From seed they come very easily, but in forms less satisfactory than those of the best named varieties. I have purchased these several times and established them here, but they have quite often produced only short stems, a real defect of proportion, since the flowers of the newer varieties are very large. Many have persisted for years, but they have never given the show gardeners get in Oregon or Washington. Oddly enough, a number of self-sown seedlings of orange shades have come up recently and have done better than plants carefully nurtured elsewhere. It may be that seedlings, established when very young, that is, set out in fall from summer-sown seed, may give better results. Named varieties are increased commercially by root cuttings and in private gardens by root division, both made when the foliage dies down after flowering.

Years ago the main objection to oriental poppies was the difficulty of harmoniously associating the typical orange with other colors. This has been overcome, for there are now named varieties of apricot, red, pink, rose, and even white. My experience with seed from a good pale pink was that a large proportion of the seedlings resembled the parent. If your conditions are promising, it is worth testing out oriental poppies. A minor species, P. pilosum, from Greece, might also be tried. Raised from seed it has proved perennial and generous in its spring show of two-inch orange flowers on stems about two feet high, an admittedly less exciting thing but with a less exacting disposition here.

PENSTEMON

Californians have considerable compensation in the ease with which they can grow penstemons, particularly that garden race of disputed parentage but certainly western Americans. After an English education, these have been returned to us, thoroughly adapted to our gardens, but with their foxglove- or gloxinia-shaped flowers greatly increased in size and wonderfully varied in color from white and pink to red and light and dark purple, many with pure white throats. The tall spikes of flowers are produced on plants suggestive of perennial phlox in their clean green ovate-lanceolate leaves.

These penstemons are rarely found in eastern American catalogs as the plants are not hardy enough to stand severe winters, but they are reasonably long-lived perennials in our gardens, asking for little but good garden soil, a sunny situation and, naturally, summer watering as summer is their season of blooming. Some English specialists offer named varieties, as with perennial phlox, but it is quite sufficient to get a good strain of seed, sow it in flats in early spring, prick out the seedlings, grow them on, then plant them out about eighteen inches apart where they will flower in late summer and autumn. Next year they will be large plants, with many spikes valuable all summer for garden decoration but not—I would add for the consolation of those who have their plants ravaged for indoor decoration—for cutting, as the flowers immediately flag when removed from the plants. Any particularly nice color or favored form can easily be perpetuated by making three-inch cuttings in summer—with a heel or below a node—from the short new growths which come after the flowers have been cut back. In this way it is possible to make border groups of several plants of the same color, a real asset when only mixtures are available. Plants can be kept strong and floriferous for some time if cut back slightly after the main flowering, and again, harder, in early spring; eventually they die of old age. Plants are sometimes infested in midsummer by a small black worm like a hairless caterpillar, which develops out of a sort of gray cobwebby mist. Any arsenic poison will kill the pests off quickly if applied when they first appear.

I also grow and recommend trial of some of our native penstemon species. My favorite, and it self-sows here, is Penstemon heterophyllus, low growing, drought-resistant, with blue flowers, easily raised from seed, and adapted to the front of borders or even to rock gardens. Carl Purdy offers plants of a selected variety called California Blue Bedder. For variety, try P. centranthifolius, the scarlet bugler, a taller, rather casual-growing drought-resistant species, with nice narrow scarlet tubular flowers. There are also others, obtainable as plants or easily raised from seed distributed by specialists in native material.

PHLOX

Hardy perennial phlox is certainly the feature of many American gardens in midsummer and an essential constituent of all hardy herbaceous borders in suitable climates. Unfortunately California is not one of these. The garden race—we can profitably forget about the species from which it is derived—naturally has the preference of its wild ancestors of the eastern half of the United States for rich moist soil, warm and wet summers, a winter in which to rest. Where such conditions can be approximated, artificially here, a considerable degree of success is possible in California. In Berkeley, Inverness, Piedmont, and Montebello, just east of Los Angeles, I have seen fine midsummer shows of phlox, good clumps of green healthy foliage and great heads of flowers, white, pink, lavender, rose, red, and purple, many of the florets with darker eyes.

In Miss Cora Brandt's warm level garden near Berkeley, well fertilized and well watered all summer, phlox give such satisfaction that plantings are being increased each year and new varieties added. She finds them "most grateful of summer perennials, so that for two months the whole garden is a blaze of vivid color, with sporadic bloom over an even longer period." She finds phlox "tolerant of both sun and light shade, so long as it has plenty of water and heavy feedings of manure and leaf mold." Some of her original plants were from my own garden, where they were no great asset, undoubtedly because they resented our dry hillside, our feeble feeding, and our lack of consideration for their great need of summer water.

If you are minded to grow perennial phlox, buy plants. It would take a lifetime of selection to raise from seed varieties of the high standard of the present fine named ones. Miss Brandt picks out Apollo, pure white; La Vague, lavender; the pinks Daily Sketch, Mrs. Milly van Hoboken, and Painted Lady, all different; among rose shades, Thor and Mrs. Sydney Mitchell, the latter a fine seedling of Hugh Logan's; in reds, Africa and Leo Schlagater; and one white with a red eye, Count Zeppelin. But the best way is to select from catalogs listing many varieties. Set out plants in fall or spring about eighteen inches apart, as they need room to spread and are best left for three or four years to form clumps, during which time bone meal and rotted cow manure will keep them vigorous. When too close or failing in growth or flower, dig up and divide the clumps, giving preference in replanting to newer outer sections with good roots. Commercially they are increased mainly by root cuttings, but division usually meets an amateur's needs. If you can give phlox what they want, they will enrich your California garden; if you can't, then leave them alone.

PRIMROSES

A book would be needed to consider primroses adequately. A paper by Professor W. C. Blasdale, "The Primula Treasure-house," in the October 1941 issue of the *Journal of the California Horticultural Society,* might serve as an introduction to the family pending the publication of his book. I shall limit myself to a few primroses which can readily be grown outdoors in California under ordinary garden conditions.

The English primrose and the hybrid race in part developed

from it, the polyanthus primroses, claim first place. Whether you give your attention to the primitive forms with single flowers on a stem or to the sturdier, showier, more effective garden polyanthus is a matter of taste. The former appear better in natural plantings, in rock gardens, and in places where their smaller, daintier, wilder-looking flowers on smaller plants with shorter stems seem more appropriate or more appealing to the gardener than their opulent relatives, with larger foliage, longer stems, and huge heads of many big flowers in a range of colors now being greatly widened from the earlier whites, yellows, and reds. There are some fine strains of polyanthus, mainly English, like the Munstead yellows and whites, and Sutton's Brilliant Mixture of reds and oranges, but the latest and to me most exciting developments are going on in California where Frank Reinelt is developing the Pacific strain. Not only have larger, stronger plants with stiffer stems and larger flowers been achieved in the older colors, but lovely bronzes, apricots, pinks, roses, blues, and blends are in process of selection, to the ultimate betterment of this flower for general garden use, for bedding, for borders, even for cutting.

The culture of both single and polyanthus primroses is much the same. They are best raised from seed, particularly the bunch-flowered ones, and this, if sown in early summer in flats of any light mixture, say half leaf mold and half garden soil, will give plants to flower the following spring. Keep the soil damp and covered until germination, remembering primroses like shade and moisture. After transference to other flats, they are ready to go into the garden by fall, where they should have at least half shade. Polyanthus particularly are heavy feeders, and in spring a quick-acting fertilizer like the unpleasant smelling fish meal or cottonseed meal will give better growth and bigger flowers, though with well-prepared soil, into which old manure has been dug, good results can be obtained without overmuch attention later.

Primroses love water all winter, and have been best with us when we had lots of rain in January and February, their desires differing altogether from those of our winter tourists. First flowerings are as good as you will ever get, and after a second season when clumps get crowded, it is best to divide and replant them; this should be done right after flowering, often not a convenient time, and the plants should be watered all through the following summer; fall dividing is far less effective if you want the best results next spring. Those fortunate enough to have lath houses will find that the partial shade and wind protection these give are ideal for the flowering of primroses. I cannot too strongly recommend the newer polyanthus varieties for the decoration of spring gardens or for the beauty of individual forms.

Primula malacoides, the fairy primrose, is certainly the next in popularity in California, and its use for bedding or for cool spring borders in half shade has greatly increased with the remarkable developments from the original small, thin-petaled pale lavender flowers to present-day varieties in white, pink, rose, red, lavender, and violet. There are even double forms, for which I have less enthusiasm. These larger, more effective varieties come fairly true from good strains of seed, and that is the way to get them, though sometimes young seedling plants are offered. Grown as a greenhouse plant in colder climates, Primula malacoides is invariably treated as a biennial in California, the seed sown in flats in August and the plants placed where they are to flower through the spring months. Afterwards it is best to discard them and begin again. We should take advantage of our cool, not cold, winters to grow more of these easy primroses.

The third garden race, not wild species, which a few favored California gardeners—I am not among them—may grow, are the really lovely candelabra primroses, derived from such species as P. japonica, P. pulverulenta, P. Beesiana, and P. Bulleyana, all with tall stems and having successive tiers of flowers which suggest the name given them and their hybrids in white, yellow, buff, orange, pink, rose, red, and purple, to mention the range of color available in these candelabras. I cannot give them what they want, damp, almost boglike soil, cool air, and lots of overhead watering, but Hugh Logan in his Inverness garden raised them readily outdoors. And in the Strybing Arboretum in cool Golden Gate Park, in a light moist soil, with lots of water from sprinklers, they make a wonderful show late every spring. Best raised from seed, they are only for adventurous gardeners or for those who can give them adequate moisture, and that means a lot of water.

PYRETHRUM

We only occasionally see pyrethrums growing in California gardens, perhaps because we have many other perennials which offer single daisies in several colors. In Washington and British Columbia, as in England, pyrethrums are grown more and are particularly valued for the hardy herbaceous border and for cutting. In late spring their single or double daisies in pink, rose, and red are bright and give variety to a planting. It is somewhat of a drawback that they have but one good season of flowering. Singles can be raised readily from seed and will come into flower the following year. Selected named varieties I do not find in American lists, nor are such doubles as the soft pink Queen Mary—which I admired in a Vancouver garden—apparently available. Once you have them, pyrethrums can be increased by division of the clumps in autumn or spring, preferably the former.

ROMNEYA COULTERI, THE MATILIJA POPPY

The Matilija poppy, Romneya Coulteri, which the great English gardener, William Robinson, called "the fairest plant that ever came to our land from that country of flowers, California," is another instance of greater appreciation abroad than at home. This drought-resistant perennial with attractive blue-green foliage and many large and beautiful May to July flowers—their crinkly white petals surround a center of golden orange stamens—is rarely seen in our modern gardens, though it grows luxuriantly in old places in the Santa Clara Valley. As a tall and permanent plant it looks well in the back of large borders and in separate groups on large places.

From much experience with the Matilija poppy in the Santa Barbara Botanic Garden, Maunsell Van Rensselaer has discussed it thoroughly in the April 1945 issue of the *Journal of the California Horticultural Society*. It is difficult to grow from seed, but propagation is feasible from root cuttings or divisions of old clumps after the first rains in late autumn. Rooted sections can be moved safely if they are severed by a spade a week or two before the transplanting and a firm ball of soil retained around them. In California, nursery plants supplied in cans are best planted out in winter or early spring. These poppies require full sun and a well-drained soil, and can do without summer water though deep irrigation will prolong blooming. The plants may be cut to the ground every autumn before the first rains. If you have the space, do not be dissuaded from growing this glorious native by the materially minded who remark on the resemblance of its flowers to fried eggs.

RUDBECKIA OR CONEFLOWERS

Rudbeckias, commonly called coneflowers because their central disks are conical, have both annual and perennial members. Of the perennials, I have grown Rudbeckia speciosa (R. Newmanii), three feet high, with dull brownish centers surrounded by long dark-yellow toothed petals, and also some mixed R. hirta hybrids, raised from seed which produced bronze, brown, and reddish as well as yellow and orange forms. One rarely sees in California the double form of R. laciniata, the tough six-foot-high hardy perennial with yellow chrysanthemumlike flowers which was introduced in the nineties and flourished mightily. It is worth trial here, growing in any ordinary soil but wanting summer water. Rudbeckias are not fine flowers, but they are easy, showy, and useful for their midsummer flowers. Rudbeckia purpurea is properly Echinacea purpurea. Its flowers, purplish rose with darker cones, are unusual and, since it is almost four feet high, easy to grow, and also a midsummer bloomer, it is worth consideration. These are all western Americans from the prairies and tablelands, and they need no coddling. The single rudbeckias come easily from seed or may be obtained as plants and increased by division.

SALVIA

Salvias, that is sages, are less grown in their varied perennial forms than their ease of growth, season of flower, and drought resistance would seem to justify. California gardeners too often know only Salvia splendens, the blinding red bedder grown, I remember, in front of the Stanford Quad, where "the color of life is red." For late flowers I have tried S. azurea and its much deeper blue variety, S. azurea grandiflora, often listed as S. Pitcheri. In later summer, they both produce three-foot racemes of small blue flowers in their different shades, when there is little of that color. The Mexican bush salvia, S. leucantha, with grayish, rather persistent lanceolate foliage, white beneath, and two-foot-high white and red-violet flowers, seems imperishable under any neglect and continues to flower till late in autumn. I have also grown, from seed, Salvia farinacea in its improved form, Blue Bedder, with shiny green foliage and deep blue flowers; it was less perennial than the others, but its flowers lasted better than the pure gentian blue but evanescent ones of S. patens. Perennial sages come easily from seed and from divisions. All they want is ordinary soil, sun, and some water in summer.

SANTOLINA AND SCABIOSA

Santolina Chamaecyparissus (S. incana)—better call it lavender-cotton and let it go at that—is valuable in the border just for its finely divided persistent gray foliage and its pleasant aromatic lavender odor; it is an edging plant which can always be kept neat and within bounds by clipping. Its yellow daisylike flowers are a liability rather than an asset and are best removed in bud in order to maintain a solid gray effect. It is quite hardy here and readily propagated by cuttings of the new growth; being drought-resistant, it is perfectly adapted to our conditions.

The perennial scabious, Scabiosa caucasica, is a flower of some value in the garden, but because it lacks a season of mass bloom it is far more useful for cutting. I had paid little attention to it until I saw at a London show an exhibit of a greatly superior strain developed by an English seedsman, Isaac House.

The flowers were lovely, not like the formal and crabbed pin-cushions of the annual scabious, but with flattish heads three inches or more across, the central boss being framed with broad petals of light to dark blue, including attractive powdery shades. I bought a packet of the then expensive seed and from it got thirteen plants, some of which I still have. Scabious are not as easy to raise from seed as some perennials. The seed must be absolutely fresh—late summer is the best time to get and sow it—and the soil must be kept comparatively dry, pending the slow and rather stingy germination. American seedsmen now offer the House strain grown in this country, but I do not know if the high standard has been maintained. Select a sunny well-drained place in the garden for the plants, which are best left undisturbed for years, and dress the soil with lime if it is lacking in that preference of the scabious. In planting do not bury the crowns or they may rot out. Flowers are most frequent in early summer, and though drought-resistant, the plants will thrive and keep in bloom much longer if watered in our dry season. Besides the blues there are white forms, but my whites from plants bought at a local nursery, are inferior to the blues. If you can find a nurseryman with a fine strain of Scabiosa caucasica, by all means buy plants. Scabiosa columbaria, is also nice, with smaller light pink or mauve flowers, blooming best in southern California in winter and, like S. caucasica, a little ragged in the garden but a good provider of cut flowers. It is a better-natured plant perhaps, but to me distinctly a second-choice scabious. Both seed and plants are offered in California.

STATICE AND THALICTRUM

Many sea lavenders or statices are annual, but there is one perennial, still commonly called Statice latifolia (though reclassified by the botanists as Limonium latifolium), of real value, particularly in dry sunny gardens. Its large panicles of lavender-blue flowers on two-foot stems are decorative on the evergreen plants or when cut, as they are dry and almost everlasting. Statice latifolia may be raised from seed, but is easier to obtain from nurseries where plants may be bought in cans.

Of the thalictrums, meadow-rues, it is not the wild ones of damp eastern American meadows which are commonly grown in California gardens, but Thalictrum dipterocarpum from western China, a taller plant, with the pleasant columbinelike foliage of the family and with graceful panicles of rosy lavender flowers showing conspicuous yellow stamens; there is also a less commonly found white form. This is undoubtedly the best species for California, as it is better adapted to our conditions, though even here it wants a cool shady place, with not over half sun, and a rich moist soil, which is worth providing, for the garden effect of this meadow-rue is fine, and the flowers are also valuable to lighten flower arrangements. It is easily raised from seed, and plants are occasionally obtainable. When away from home, I have envied gardeners who could grow, in Boston or in Seattle, the several nice feathery garden forms of the European Thalictrum aquilegifolium, less tall but perhaps for that reason a better garden plant than the Chinese species, but its absence from California gardens indicates that it really requires more moisture than we can give it, and perhaps more winter cold as well.

TROLLIUS OR GLOBE FLOWER

It is hard for a good-natured gardener, as it is for a similar parent, to have to keep saying don't, but of course I do not have to be obeyed. If you enjoyed attractive clumps of globe flowers or trollius, with great double yellow or orange blooms like glorified buttercups—particularly appreciated in Maine or Minnesota because they flower so early—I can only say don't expect a comparable thrill from them in California. They are from cold regions, mostly swampy places, and they insist on moist soil. Moreover they have too much spirited competition in their season here from their gorgeous relatives, the ranunculus.

VALERIANA

Valeriana officinalis, the hardy garden heliotrope, I cherished as a child for its early summer pinkish white flowers on tall airy stems, and particularly for its fragrance where it did not have to compete with real heliotrope as a garden perennial. I doubt its worth here. What we call valerian was once Valeriana coccinea or V. rubra, and is now botanically Centranthus ruber, but by neither name is it sweet. It is a Mediterranean perennial, growing about three feet high, with, in the typical form, panicles of virulent pink or bluish rose. There is an equally unpleasant dirty white variety and a light red one which is innocuous, even worth growing in some situations. All forms are so tough and drought-resistant, and they self-sow so readily that they may be seen growing in walls and waste places without care. If I wanted any, I would look for the red form, propagate it by division, and destroy all seedlings which appeared.

VERBASCUM AND VERONICA

Verbascums, or mulleins, are not plants of prime importance, but their large grayish leaves and tall spikes of yellow or purple, or in the newer hybrids, old rose, pink, or white, are useful for breaking the uniformity of level in a border and for giving variety. They are mostly biennials, flowering from seed the season after sowing, but in California—so like Greece from which many of them come—they are drought-resistant and tend to self-sow, asking nothing but a warm sunny place.

Veronicas, or speedwells, are better known in California by the numerous shrubby ones from New Zealand, which are now classed as Hebe and have already been discussed under Evergreen Shrubs. The dwarfer herbaceous kinds fit best in rock gardens; the taller ones, mostly forms of Veronica spicata, have two-foot spikes of violet-blue flowers and may be considered for middle-border plantings. I grew the species, V. spicata, in the east where it was easy and permanent, but here it is rarely seen. Being from northern Europe, perhaps it wants more summer moisture than gardeners give their borders here. It is distinct and pleasant, though hardly exciting.

VIOLAS

Viola is the botanical name of a wide variety of plants, but only the garden violas, derivatives of Viola cornuta, and the sweet-scented garden violets, so prized for corsages, will be considered here.

Even garden violas vary considerably in habit. Visitors to English gardens or to those in the Pacific northwest are always attracted by the lovely self shades of the tufted or bedding pansies, better called bedding violas. The beautiful lavender Maggie Mott and the fine yellow Moseley Perfection are good examples. I have imported some from the north, but for success I also should have imported the Puget Sound climate—too big a price for Californians to pay. Perhaps along the cool coast, in level gardens with rich soil and plenty of water, these violas may be fairly successful, but I suggest raising them from seed rather than getting named varieties propagated by cuttings, for they seem more vigorous so raised and many good colors are available, white, yellow, lovely apricot, bronze, ruby, mauve, and violet. American violas, bred apparently for our drier, warmer summers, have less luscious flowers which are smaller and narrower, but they are easier and far more persistent. Jersey Gem and many others raised by specialists and available in plants only are well worth a place for edging borders or for bedding; in California they grow best in partial shade, perhaps on the east side of the house. They like a rich loose soil, plenty of water all summer, and attention to removing seed pods and cutting back straggling branches. They can be rooted from stem cuttings of short stout unflowered pieces, late summer being the best time to do this.

VIOLETS

The fragrant violets are far easier and more perennial, but less effective as garden plants, having proportionately larger leaves and smaller flowers. Every gardener in California can have a try at a patch for cutting or a certain wild garden effect which they give when happy. They are more drought-resistant than most violas, but they have certain needs for success which are easier to supply along the coast than in hot dry inland gardens. Their preference is for shade, not too dense, or they will produce only leaves. They should not be grown under pines or acacias, which leave them little or none of the essential moisture. They prefer a rich loamy soil into which a good deal of leaf mold has been dug. Plants are best obtained in fall and set about a foot apart, as they stool out and also increase from runners. These should be removed carefully in late summer whether wanted or not for new plantings. After flowering, cultivation is simple; water until summer sets in and then give the plants a rest. Fertilizing should be moderate as it may result in more leaves than flowers. A top dressing of leaf mold or bone flour dug in during autumn is usually adequate. Don't let plants get crowded; every few years they should be lifted in autumn, divided, and replanted to single crowns in new and well-prepared soil. This is of course the way to grow fine violets, but they can be grown casually for ground cover under flowering fruit trees. In our garden the white especially has self-sown and run wild.

Among older varieties available is Princess of Wales, a very large single violet blue with delicate odor and long stems. Its later development is Lady Lloyd George, large and fragrant and an improvement on its parent. Very large for a sweet-scented violet is the still newer Royal Robe, a fine variety for California conditions. A grower near Santa Cruz has announced the Victory Violet, which she says has flowers a couple of inches across, with leaves which average six inches in width. Among widely distributed violets of less usual color are Rosina, pink and rose and quite fragrant, and American Beauty, red, and very hardy but less fragrant. In white singles, the Czar is fragrant and prolific, ramps all over here, and is nice for contrast and bunching. Among the double violets, Marie Louise, mauve with a lighter center and fragrant, the old Neapolitan Violet (syn. De Parme), much grown for perfume makers, and the white Swanley, fragrant and on six-inch stems, afford ample choice.

YUCCA

Yucca filamentosa, the Adams-needle of the old gardens, is the only one of the large family of this American native which

I have grown. It is a bold plant with swordlike foliage from which in midsummer in California come three-foot stalks with striking panicles of many large creamy white bells, drooping gracefully from the branched candelabralike stem. Here in ordinary soil and full sun it does well with little water. It is an effective plant in itself and might be useful to give accent in the rear of a big border by reason of its summer season of bloom.

ZAUSCHNERIA

Zauschneria californica, the so-called California fuchsia, coming at the end of the alphabet, enables me to complete this long chapter with a native perennial, not really a fuchsia, but an almost evergreen herbaceous plant of casual growth but easy, persistent, and, in our garden, indifferent to summer moisture. Its value lies in its complete adaptability to our conditions and its display of scarlet tubular flowers from late summer on, lasting long into autumn, not a fine or spectacular plant, but by fall we are tired of prima donnas and appreciate this native for its good nature. Any rooted piece of an old plant can be separated and replanted in fall or spring, or it may be raised from seed obtainable from specialists in our natives.

CHAPTER NINE

IRISES

T IS proper that the tall bearded irises should be discussed first, for they are a feature of many California gardens in April and May their season being twice as long here as in colder climates. These irises demand sun, not necessarily all day, but at least for half of it, and they are the better for more. They will grow in considerable shade but produce leaves with no flowers, so give them an open sunny place. They also demand good drainage. On a slope they will get it naturally, but in a level garden drainage should be furnished, particularly if much summer watering reaches the plants. Concerning soils, irises are more amenable, but they seem to have a preference for the heavier and richer loams, so if you have Alameda or Carmel or similar sand, it will have to be strengthened or fertilized fairly heavily. In California you can plant these irises whenever soil conditions permit, but I prefer to do it between the time they finish flowering, say early June, and the time heavy rains set in, which is generally in November. If set out in early summer, the plants will need occasional watering to establish them through the dry season, while later planted ones can largely depend on natural rainfall. A soil in which irises have not recently been grown, that is, a soil new to them, has always seemed preferable to me, but is not always available.

Fertilizers are best incorporated into the soil before planting; old cow manure or bone meal thoroughly mixed in the soil beneath the rhizomes is hard to beat. Ammophos is recommended by some growers. It is dug in in late fall or early spring, or a complete commercial fertilizer lightly hoed in between plants is used as a stimulant. With good soil to start with, I have found I could get excellent results without much fertilizer, but I am, I fear, a poor provider.

In planting, use good single rhizomes, not clumps, and spread the roots well but barely cover the fleshy rhizomes, which enjoy a sun baking; burying them deeply invites rhizome rot. Even if several plants of a variety are desired together for a mass effect, plant rhizomes singly and so arrange them that the green growing ends radiate from a center, or so alternate them that they will not run into each other as growth goes on from year to year. The flower stems come out of the center of each fan after side shoots are produced; the side shoots carry on and flower the following year. The appearance of a new planting is a bit thin the first year but should be at its best in the second and third seasons, after which either thinning out or replanting is desirable for the more vigorous varieties. Thinning out may consist of the removal of atrophied rhizomes with a chisel or similar tool, or the lifting and replanting elsewhere of crowded growths of potential blooming capacity. Thinning must eventually give place to a thorough soil change, a renovation and complete replanting, for which no definite time can be set.

Watering of newly set plants is desirable if the soil is dry, and this should be continued in moderation until autumn, but in the cool coastal regions of California established plantings can get through long summer droughts without much watering, though an occasional soaking does them no harm and is particularly desirable in the warmer sections of the state. Watering certainly helps to improve stems and flowers when late spring rains fail us, but care should be taken not to overwater irises recently planted or those which are in a state of rest. Always pick a cool spell for watering, not midday, and not in the midst of a warm wave. Heat and water favor iris rhizome rot.

From iris diseases or pests we are practically immune in California—no winterkilling, no borer, and little of the rhizome rot, which is commoner however in summers of heat and rain. If this does appear—evidenced by a soft mushy condition at the base of the flower stem or center of the rhizome—lift the affected plants, cut out soft parts, steep the rhizomes in a rose-red solution of potassium permanganate, dry them out in the sun for a few days, and replant. Sometimes new leafage in spring is unattractively spotted, a condition due to warm muggy weather. To keep spotting in check would involve fairly continuous spraying with winter Bordeaux or other specifics, and unless you are a perfectionist it may not be worth the trouble. It does not kill the plant, though it does temporarily disfigure it.

IRISES IN THE GARDEN PICTURE

While the interest of many growers of tall bearded irises is unquestionably in the individual flower, the concern of more general gardeners is with their contribution to the garden picture. If they are grown at all, they cannot be overlooked, their upright flower stems, their gay and glamorous colors, even their distinct foliage preclude any pretensions of modesty; they do not propose to blush unseen. In smaller gardens particularly—

and it was in these that I grew them for many years—it is important to realize their liabilities as well as their assets. Their season, though not short, cannot compare with the very long one of certain summer flowers. It is therefore some advantage to segregate irises in one corner or area, preferably not in the immediate vicinity of the house. Then a suitable and effective grouping can be made, with consideration to the varying heights of the varieties, the size of their flowers, and the color combinations which are most pleasing. From much experience I recommend for such garden use a few clumps of perhaps three or five plants each, rather than single specimens of many more varieties, which, if more interesting, are also more restless in effect.

For larger gardens and particularly where irises are to be the feature of late spring, segregation is essential, but two main types of arrangement are possible—the iris border and the iris garden, with both of which I have experimented. Either may be effective. A double border of iris is preferable to a single one and is more feasible under average conditions than, for instance, a single border of gladiolus or daffodils or any other flowers which tend to face the sun rather than to blossom all around the stems. There should be enough space to make strong groups of many varieties and to include both those varieties suited to backgrounds and those with subtle colorings or complicated patterns, like the plicatas, better seen close at hand, that is, along the path.

As the iris is a flower of light, and its beauty is enhanced by the slanting rays of the sun shining in the morning or late afternoon through the petals, heavy evergreen backgrounds are unnecessary to borders and may even be detrimental to their effect. In California, where the midday sun is garish, it is well to remember that iris borders are not at their best around noon, that colors are loveliest under more tempered light.

A separate iris garden is best placed where it will be inconspicuous when out of flower but not too far away when you and your visitors want to see it. A separate flat area, hemmed in by pergola, trellis, or shrubbery, and cut up into beds or borders by paths providing close access to all varieties would be one solution. Another would be the selection of an amphitheater on the sloping margin of a property where from the entrance a full view would be obtainable of the massed planting, semicircular and cross paths again giving access to the different varieties. I saw such an iris garden in Victoria, B. C., up above the rear of a house on the site of an old tennis court which had gone out of use. It was really quite accessible, but also easily disregarded, and as good a solution of the iris problem as I had ever seen.

These tall bearded irises can also be used in herbaceous or in mixed borders of perennials and annuals, where they are best considered, I believe, as accent points, that is, separate groups somewhat evenly spaced through the border and each of a single variety. The size of the clumps should be in proportion to the dimensions of the whole border, that is, a proper relationship should be maintained. Culturally such plantings are quite possible, for if drainage is good, a reasonable amount of water in summer will not hurt them and may even benefit irises in warm areas; but care should be taken not to let them get waterlogged. It is also necessary for future flowering to leave the rhizomes open to the sunlight and not permit them to be covered or shadowed by the rank foliage of other perennials or of such rampant annuals as petunias or nasturtiums. If while new plantings are thin, it is desirable to associate some

154

annual with them, it should be a slender upright grower like linaria or larkspur, with the seed sown thinly between the irises.

A recommended selection of varieties of irises needs to be offered with reservations. It is really best to pick out what suits your own taste or meets your own needs by visiting nurseries or private gardens with good collections, but it must always be recognized that both commercial growers and amateur specialists tend to emphasize novelties. These, because the available supply is below demand, remain expensive for some years and the general gardener can often get equally satisfactory effects from older well-tried varieties which have become standard because they have survived. I am therefore giving two sets of selections, the first of inexpensive older varieties still listed in California catalogs and mostly of California origin, as is natural, for a great deal of good breeding has been done here. On the whole these are tall varieties with large flowers and better suited to rear or middle locations than to the front of any planting. It is regrettable that many nice irises with stems of medium height and smaller flowers are no longer generally available; their scarcity is the only reason I omit them. It may be noticed that the majority of my selections are of the lighter colors. For garden use, these are far more effective than dark somber shades. Moreover in any large planting, many whites, creams, and pale yellows should be included to prevent harsh combinations of adjacent colors and to blend the whole picture together.

Among whites, Purissima, though nearly twenty years old, is still outstanding, very tall and very early; it is particularly good planted alone as it often blooms too early for grouping with others and is almost too much of an individualist to mix with them. A couple of smaller less pure whites of my own breeding, Bridal Veil and Natividad, are better for association, being of medium season, height, and size of flower. Carved Ivory is another fine big near-white. For a white effect the paler plicatas can also be used, and Los Angeles is still unbeaten, though I remember its first flowering twenty-two years ago. Snoqualmie is a lovely cream. Among low-priced yellows those most sold by one large commercial iris garden happen to be three which I raised in the early thirties—Happy Days, a huge pale yellow of great vigor and very free-flowering habit; California Gold, a strong deeper shade; and Naranja, a real orange, as its name indicates. All three have been superseded by varieties of clearer color and finer form, but these are still expensive.

Of blues and lavenders for California, Shining Waters is my first choice among older varieties in the paler shades, Sierra Blue in considerably deeper tones, and San Diego or Brunhilde in the darker blues, the latter of better color but of less dependable quality in my experience. Missouri is another excellent medium blue and Persia is suggested as a blue-gray bicolor blend, very distinct and happy here. There are no true pink irises even among the novelties, but approaches to pink exist. Among the older ones, Frieda Mohr and Miss California are still most commonly grown here.

Among standard varieties approaching the yellow and red of the old variegatas, Frank Adams is as good as any. Bronzino is still more of a blend of these colors, and the French introduction Jean Cayeux is the forerunner of many café-au-lait or light brown irises. In the darker reds or purples I think I would select Dauntless—a better doer than my own larger Rubeo—

and Dark Knight and the New Zealander, Destiny. Varieties of a dark velvety purple tend to burn under our sunshine and fog.

Novelties live a hard life. Many of them are merely claimants like "the most desirable debutante" or "the best-dressed American woman" of the year. Some in time will become the standards to replace many of those I have just mentioned. Here are a few which I have selected for trial or use in breeding. Many are rather costly for any but the specialist.

SELECTION OF NOVELTIES

Among white novelties I select Mt. Washington and the beautifully frilled Snow Flurry, both tall, and Priscilla, low and more nearly all white than any I have seen; among plicatas, Blue Shimmer, a lovely color, and Love Affair, one of my own varieties with a pinkish edge to its white ground; and among cream or yellow-grounded ones, I would choose Ruth Pollock, low-growing here but colorful. There are better ones coming on everywhere. Wabash is still the highest rating of amoena coloring, that is, with white standards and purple falls, but it too will be superseded. Great Lakes is still tops in light blue, and Chivalry in deep medium blue. For violets I suggest the lovely low Amigo and the rich Deep Velvet. Of the so-called pinks, China Maid, Pink Reflection, Remembrance, and Daybreak form a fair selection in the lighter shades, and Orchid Lady, Inspiration, Dream Castle, and Mulberry Rose in the darker ones. Real pinks are now in the making. I feel less competent to select reds, but Christabel and Red Valor have met general favor, and in the browner tones Solid Mahogany is the best. The yellow and red bicolors can stand improvement, but for the time I want the low but lovely Mexico and the tall Gay

Senorita. In yellows my choice is the pale Golden Fleece, the two-toned Fair Elaine, and Golden Madonna, Golden Majesty, Berkeley Gold, and Ola Kala. It is hard to make a selection from the yellow and brown blends, but it must include Prairie Sunset; I would add Pacific Sunset and Tobacco Road and many more if I did not hold myself in. From the descendants of the wonderful hybrid William Mohr, two—Elmohr and Lady Mohr—are indispensable. This selection of novelties is based wholly on experience under my own conditions.

DWARFS AND INTERMEDIATES

Two groups of bearded irises, both admittedly of minor importance for California gardens, are the dwarfs and the intermediates. After I came to California I sent east for the collection of dwarfs I had gathered together. But I reluctantly realized that these miniatures loomed larger in the garden plans of those in cold climates who cherished them because they were early and thus lengthened the bearded iris season; in California they had to compete with the earlier tall bearded varieties like Purissima and San Gabriel. True, the dwarfs and intermediates did make pleasant patches, low on the ground on sunny slopes, and they were gay and colorful for their short season, but they were not in flower for more than a couple of weeks of our long garden year and their foliage was not very interesting, moreover they needed a lot of tiresome hand weeding and fairly frequent moving, so they were given away or allowed to die out. Perhaps some Californians with different gardens, in which these lower irises would be in better scale, may want to try them, as they are very easy to grow. I note that Carl Starker, Jennings Lodge, Oregon, offers by far the largest collection, over fifty varieties, with a good many doubtless rather similar. The intermediates, from crosses between the tall and the dwarf bearded irises, come in a rather limited color range. I gave these up earlier as being inferior to the taller ones, whose season they overlap, and not having the special use in rock gardens of the dwarfs. I now have only Snow Maiden, a white I can recommend.

ONCOCYCLUS AND REGELIAS

Over fifty years ago a middle-aged woman sat in the open section of one of our world-famous California Street cable cars as it climbed over Nob Hill. With one of the finest views of San Francisco Bay before the passengers, they all turned to look at the bunch of strange flowers she held in her hand. Those were leisurely days, so to avoid crowding and accidents, the car was stopped to give everyone a look, and Mrs. Jemima Brannin, a grand old gardener, who died only a few years ago in her middle nineties, showed them Iris susiana with huge rounded flowers of white ground so covered with black and deep purple lines that they looked like big gray plumes, a somber sight. Many years later it was occasionally possible to find bunches of them in March in the more enterprising flower shops, but now they are rarely seen there or in our gardens. Iris susiana is the commonest and most easily grown of the oncocyclus irises, flowers of weird beauty from Palestine, Armenia, and the eastern Mediterranean. I had a few at one time, but they are fickle flowers, coming from places where they can be dormant in winter and baked in summer. They are certainly worth trying if you can get them, especially if you have their preferred conditions, which are available in such places as Colfax, on the west slope of our Sierras, where it is cold in winter and hot and dry in summer. Sunny aspect, raised beds of gravelly soil, and renewal by seed are suggestions for their growing, but they are specialists' flowers and rarely permanent or satisfactory in the wet open winters of the coast. It was with one of this group, Iris Gatesii, that William Mohr crossed an old bearded iris, Parisiana, and raised the famous hybrid I named for him after his death; this has become the parent of a new race of easily grown bearded irises. Elmohr and Lady Mohr are examples and others will follow, carrying something of the novelty of the difficult oncocyclus into more easily grown garden irises.

The related Regelias, comprising such species as the unusual Iris Korolkowi and I. stolonifera and the perfectly finished lavender I. Hoogiana from Turkestan, are more amenable to cultivation under ordinary garden conditions but with care as to drainage. Though smaller and narrow they are highly individual and attractive. William Mohr's Carmelo and Clarence White's Sheriffa are doubtless hybrids between Regelias and bearded irises; they are vigorous and easy.

BEARDLESS IRISES

As garden plants the tall bearded irises must retain first place, but the many beardless irises—so called because there is no line of fuzzy growth at the base of their lower petals or falls—offer certain advantages which remove them from competition. Bearded irises normally give about a month of good bloom here, but from the beardless species a selection can be made which will give flowers from early autumn right through winter and spring to midsummer. It is true the flowers (except among the Japanese iris) will be in a more limited range of color, and as the beardless irises are in the main wild forms, the flowers will have relatively narrower petals and be less sumptuous though more graceful in effect. The plants are characterized generally by a fibrous root system rather than fleshy rhizomes, but some, notably those of the spuria section and even our natives, have an approach to a rhizome, though it is narrower, tougher, and drier than in the bearded irises. It follows from their type of root that the beardless irises should not be left around to dry out. An advantage many of them have is their ability to take a good deal of summer water, thereby adapting themselves to growth among herbaceous plants and annuals. Many will thrive under less sunny conditions than bearded irises, a few flowering even in considerable shade. They seem to prefer neutral or even acid soils to those with much lime. Though relatively slow to establish they can get along with less division and replanting, some of them thriving for a decade without attention. All have comparatively narrow green leafage, generally upright in growth, which blends more easily with that of other plants than does the broad, some- times lax, often grayish foliage of the bearded irises.

In the following notes I have made a selection of species and of garden varieties almost all of which I have grown at some time or other in California. In general I have tried to arrange them in their order of flowering, beginning with the autumn and ending with the summer, but as some groups overlap in time of bloom I have tried to keep the species in the various subsections together and even, where possible, to discuss the irises of each continent at the same time.

The beardless iris season begins with, often before, the fall rains, with the flowering of I. unguicularis, also more fre- quently and easily called I. stylosa, though the jawbreaker name has priority. Perhaps one may call it the Algerian iris and let it go at that, for the earlier flowering and therefore more popular forms come from northern Africa. It is so easy to grow, so perfectly adapted to our conditions, so tolerant of different soils, that every California garden should have a patch or two of it for cutting and garden decoration. It looks well planted along a path, and I have found that it does well both in full sun and in the partial shade of an eastern exposure. The two seasons for planting or division of crowded beds are in spring: March or April after flowering, or in early autumn, September preferably, before flowering. Do not divide too small, but set out pieces of half a dozen shoots or more, at least a foot apart; they will fill the intervening spaces. Water to get the plants established, but once growing they need no attention and are better planted in a place where they will get no summer water. As they are slow to settle down to profuse flowering, do not expect a great deal for a year or two, but thereafter they will bloom each autumn, even when badly crowded. If plants are grown mainly for cut flowers, leave the foliage untrimmed and pick the blossoms in bud; they open beautifully in water. For garden effect, it is better to cut back the old foliage in September so that the spring flowers will not be hidden in it; this seems to bother the plants not at all. When, after a few years, clumps get too crowded, dig up some of them and divide and replant for future flowering, but leave some old plants to give bloom until the newer lots are well established. The commonest form of I. unguicularis is a clear lavender, varying in color depth. This is a fall bloomer. Flowering also in autumn is an inferior but quite pleasant white variety, and in late winter the more northern Cretan forms bloom, with less valued smaller, deeper purple flowers. It is surprising that so few Californians grow this iris which northern gardeners covet and the occasional flowering of which in England, after a dry summer, causes gardeners there to write to *The Times* about it.

Next in time of flowering comes the large section of irises native to California and Oregon, several of such great garden value that it is hard to explain their neglect. An understanding of their simple yet very specific needs might remedy this. I recommend first of all I. Douglasiana, native to the coast of northern California and the redwood belt, thriving on mesas and hill slopes, varying in size of flower, but identified by its strong growth of dark green foliage—which turns red as it dies in autumn—and by its stems, often eighteen inches or more high and branching, with two or three flowers in each head. The color variations seem innumerable from pure white, which is rare, through lavender and mauve to deep violet purple; there are also cream forms, often with pinkish markings.

Less luxuriant in foliage are two species found mainly in Oregon, I. bracteata and I. tenax. The former, taking its name from the bractlike leaves which clothe the stem, is a plant of scantier foliage, broad and shiny on the upper side. Flower stems are about eight inches high with single heads of two flowers, yellow, veined brown. More important as a garden plant is I. tenax, with its narrow foliage and stems a foot or so high, bearing flowers varying from red purple to mauve and lavender, with paler centers and rounded blades to the falls. Much smaller than these is I. macrosiphon, with a long distinctive perianth tube and flowers—often opening low down in the tall narrow foliage—generally deep blue purple, though red-purple forms are found; not a particularly robust plant, but it grows easily enough for me. It is found on Mt. Tamalpais and up the coast into Oregon. Also small and dainty but a better garden plant is the more recently found I. innominata from Oregon, with slender grasslike leaves and flowers, usually of a lovely warm orange, though blue forms exist, an iris more suited to the rock garden than the border and enjoying more shade and water than the tougher species from California. There are several other California species—the nomenclature is in need of revision—but they are of little garden value. Such a one is I. Hartwegii, a yellow or lavender from the Sierra; you can see it in the Yosemite Valley; it is of little more than botanical interest.

Presumably, inability to obtain these natives readily in nurseries or iris gardens is the main reason they are seen so little in our gardens. However I note that Carl Starker lists native species and selected forms. Transplanted stock or divisions of new growth in autumn or early spring seem to move pretty well. Collecting in the wild would be the easiest and most interesting way to get fine forms if it were not that these irises all resent being moved in flower. While I have transplanted them in full bloom and Hugh Logan of Inverness tells me he also has done so, my success has been best when in January, just before the beginning of growth, I removed the youngest outside single rhizomes or growths with a chisel or similar tool and replanted them without too much delay and before they had dried out. Handled in this way they move very easily. Whole clumps transplant badly. But by far the best way to get the species iris is from seed, picked when ripe in midsummer (or purchased), and sown in beds or frames in autumn. Seeds germinate readily in January or February and plants can be moved into permanent places in early summer, if there are facilities for summer watering, otherwise it is best to transplant them only after the rains commence. Seeds are offered by specialists in California natives.

The only other native California iris of garden importance is I. longipetala, a coarser, taller grower, commonly found in certain places wet in spring though dry in summer. It abounds in low areas in South San Francisco and in similar localities along the coast. The foliage is upright, the flowers generally white or gray, heavily lined and flushed blue. This iris has no cultural demands, grows anywhere I put it, never wants summer water, and moves more readily than other California species. Closely related is I. missouriensis of the western plateau and mountains, extending to our Sierra and even over into Tulare County. It is of course hardier but is not important to us, being less showy than I. longipetala and less happy in our dry summers. Here too we might mention I. versicolor, with blue and white or blue-purple, even red-purple flowers, growing in marshy lands and around the margins of ponds on the Atlantic coast. As a child in eastern Canada I often got my feet wet—and my seat warmed—picking it. In California if you want to grow it for old times' sake, it is hardly worth while otherwise, put it in any ordinary soil, say in a herbaceous border, where it will get some summer moisture; it does not demand much.

LOUISIANA NATIVES

From the Southern States, with Louisiana as the center, come a whole series of American irises native to warm climates and wet heavy soils along lakes and creeks. As a group they have long foliage, sometimes lax, more often upright, and spidery flowers, sometimes overtopped by the foliage. One, I. fulva, is very distinct in having terra-cotta colored flowers, others like I. hexagona are more ordinary in their lavender color. Of recent years in the delta of the Mississippi many new forms have been found. From these wild materials breeders have raised many hybrids now in commerce, but the finest forms still seem to be local variations or natural hybrids found in the swamps or gardens of the South, among them whites, pale blues, yellows, deep purples, and variations of these. In California these southern natives thrive best if they get water in summer. The few planted along the lawn in a neighbor's garden apparently like that situation. The conditions for growing azaleas in California have also been recommended for them. Though they may be bog or swamp irises by preference, with irrigation they can apparently be grown anywhere in California. One of the chief amateur specialists is at San Bernardino, than which we have few more desiccated districts. To me the Louisiana irises seem of secondary garden importance, but they are distinct, and as improved varieties are disseminated, they will have a value because they follow the peak of the bearded iris season here.

EVANSIA SECTION

A small group of irises, the Evansia section, have in common a crest like a cockscomb. Though not of prime garden importance, one of the species, I. japonica (syn. I. fimbriata), is occasionally grown in California, blooming in April. Its broad green polished leaves are surmounted by slender, wiry, much-branched flower stems, and the numerous flat lavender flowers with golden centers suggest orchids. It is the first iris I ever saw flowering in considerable shade, and I have learned in my own garden that it is not happy in full sun. It is a dainty plant and worth growing. So is the taller but somewhat similar I. Wattii, from southern China, which grows like a weed around Los Angeles and in warmer sections.

In this group also comes I. tectorum, so called because it is grown on the ridge of thatched roofs in Japan. In my garden its flat blue-purple flowers were so rare that I gave it up, but W. R. Dykes says it is not difficult in England if grown in fairly rich soil and well ripened in summer. The smaller crested irises like the Japanese I. gracilipes or the eastern American I. cristata are treasures for the meticulous rock gardener, as they are fussy about moisture and drainage and cannot be expected to take the rough and tumble of a casual herbaceous border.

IRIS PSEUDACORUS

Flowering with the bearded irises is a European beardless iris which does not fall into any grouping, I. pseudacorus. It is distinguished by tall, stiff, upright rushlike leaves and three-foot stems bearing yellow flowers, generally with brown markings at the base of the round falls. This is a marsh plant all over Europe, but I have found that it grows and flowers readily in the herbaceous border. Still, it does look best around pools or ponds.

SIBERIAN IRIS

Also flowering about the same time as the later bearded irises are the many forms of I. sibirica. The typical I. sibirica has tall narrow green leaves and even taller hollow stems bearing several small blue and white veined flowers of graceful form. It seems to be a native of Europe rather than Asia, but from Siberia east and into Japan there is a variety (Dykes calls it a different species), I. orientalis, which has shorter stems and larger flowers of either deep purple or white.

The Siberian iris, especially the many better garden forms raised by plant breeders, are fine border plants of easy culture.

From my experience in growing them on the Atlantic coast, I am sure they are happier and more vigorous there where they get from natural rainfall the moisture they like; but in our dry California summers, if they are given a good deal of irrigation the first year or two while they are getting established, they will do very well. You do not have to have such a swampy place for them as their location in the Japanese Tea Garden in Golden Gate Park. Division of crowded clumps and new plantings are best made in autumn. Give the Siberians preferably a rich soil. A manure mulch will help to retain moisture and also feed them. Until so crowded they fail to flower well, leave them alone as they are happiest when undisturbed. Of the older kinds, Perry's Blue in the paler shades, Emperor in purple blue, and Snow Queen, a white, are the best selections. There are, however, even better, newer ones, including Gatineau, a tall light blue; Caesar's Brother, a very dark purple; and Snow Crest, the best white. Recently red-purple forms have been offered, but I have not tried them here. The first three are all doing well even on my dry hillside where I do soak them sometimes in summer.

SPURIAS

To the last lot to be considered, the group name of spurias has been given, though the species I. spuria, translatable as the bastard, is an inoffensive and unimportant blue-purple member, extending in various forms from Spain to Kashmir. This group is valuable to us because it follows the bearded irises and pretty well fills in the gap between them and the Japanese. The spurias are mostly from the eastern Mediterranean, where they have ample moisture during their growing season in winter and spring, but dry off during summer, just the conditions we have in California. They all have tall, swordlike, deep green leaves and spidery flowers—somewhat like those of the Spanish and Dutch bulbous irises—closely adhering to the sides of rigid solid stems which are often five or six feet high.

Easily the best known here is I. ochroleuca, which has white flowers with a large conspicuous yellow blotch on the falls. Very similar to it but generally preferred for its pure soft yellow color is I. Monnieri, probably, Dykes says, not a true species but a color variation of I. ochroleuca. The related species, I. aurea, is a deeper, richer yellow, but in my experience it is a less rugged plant and needs two or three years after planting to commence flowering again.

From the blue-purple I. spuria and the yellow I. Monnieri, Sir Michael Foster raised a series of hybrids, all far better than I. spuria and all in varying shades of blue. Of these I have grown Lord Wolseley and A. J. Balfour, and I can commend them as easy and pleasing garden plants. This section of iris is now under process of intensive improvement in the competent hands of Eric Nies, a Hollywood amateur, who has interbred the various species and varieties and not only achieved finer, broader, and sometimes frilled flowers in the old colors but has increased the color range, especially in bronze shades. Bronzspur, Michigan State, and Dutch Defiance are among his best varieties now available, but others not yet distributed will add to the value of this group for our gardens and for corsages.

Unlike bearded irises, the spurias do not like moving. If it is necessary, they prefer that it be done in autumn, when they are dormant but getting ready to grow. They do not flower the year following a transplanting, but in compensation they will not need moving for many years and thereafter will blossom annually with no attention whatever. Their flowers make good decorations for very large containers, the only objection being that they seem to attract ants as do no other irises.

JAPANESE IRIS

Though there are several beardless iris species from Japan, it is to the highly developed forms of Iris Kaempferi that the name Japanese irises is always applied. These garden forms—some with three hanging petals (singles), some with six (doubles)—have been developed by Japanese gardeners over many years, and additions to the extensive lists of named varieties have been made by American breeders. Many of the imported ones still retain their difficult Japanese names, a number of these have been translated, and in other cases new names have been given, so the situation is complicated, and one is not always sure of the correctness of the nomenclature. Because of this, though I grew a good collection at Stanford and still have a few, I hardly care to suggest varieties, advising rather that selection be made from plants in bloom or from the catalog descriptions of reputable growers. The range of colors is wide, from white through lavenders and deep blues to dark purples, and from lilac pinks to dark rich reds. Besides there are varieties with mottled, flecked, or other complicated color patterns, which are less effective, I think, than those with flowers of clear color. Whether one prefers the singles, which are lighter and more graceful, or the nearly flat platelike doubles, which offer a more effective expanse of color when looked down on, is a matter of taste. Cultural directions generally suggest sun or partial shade. In California where the sun is often strong in June—the height of the season for Japanese iris—it is better to give partial shade, with morning rather than afternoon sun, as individual flowers will last longer and the dark-colored varieties will not get burned and shriveled in a hot wave.

The Japanese irises prefer an acid soil to one with lime in it, and they also like a soil rich in humus and fairly retentive of moisture. One which dries out readily might be benefited by a mulch of old manure, as these irises are heavy feeders. They do not demand bog conditions, though they enjoy lots of summer water; and while they look best and thrive on the margins of pools where the water is close underneath, they can be quite successfully grown in flower borders which get regular summer waterings. The time they really require water is before and during the blooming season. The Japanese irises do not thrive on dry sunny slopes; in fact, their preferences are far removed from those of the tall bearded irises, and they cannot be treated as casually. Unless plants are obtained in cans, from which they may be set out at any time, I prefer to get new varieties or to divide old ones in the garden in early autumn or very early spring so that they do not have to face a long dry season before they are established. Leave them alone as long as they are doing well, but when they grow into big rings and need division and new rich soil, break up the old clumps into divisions of half a dozen growths rather than into single pieces, which I have found are more difficult to establish. (There is no room in gardens for prejudice, but there is a place in many of them for Japanese irises, just as there is one in opera for *Madame Butterfly*.)

BULBOUS IRIS

Irises with bulbs instead of rhizomes or fibrous roots include many almost unknown but lovely little species and also two garden groups—the Spanish-Dutch and the English irises.

The species are all earlier than the hybrids and unfortunately difficult to find in America. Theoretically, Iris alata, from Spain, North Africa, and Sicily, where it grows like a weed, should be perfectly adapted to the warmer California gardens, but though I imported bulbs from Europe after seeing it wild in Spain near Cordova and Ronda, I cannot report real success with it, nor can E. O. Orpet of Santa Barbara, a fine old gardener who ought to be able to grow it if anyone can. As with all members of the Juno section which follow, the foliage suggests miniature Indian corn, and the flowers appear from the upper axils of the leaves.

In the case of I. alata, the sweet-scented flowers open very early, in late December or January, and are a beautiful lavender blue, with one or two in a head. In my garden they have appeared off and on for several years but are now dwindling out. I suspect they want a more gravelly soil than we have or a hotter summer to ripen the bulbs. Iris bucharica, from Bokhara, is taller and later, and has more flowers, which are white with a yellow blade. It is a really easy and vigorous plant. From bulbs given me years ago, I. bucharica flowers every March, though it really gets no care at all on the crowded slope below the house, but the soil is well drained there and dry all summer. Iris sindjarensis persisted several years and seemed sturdy; its vanilla-scented pale blue flowers were watched for each spring.

The other little bulbous irises occasionally available belong to the Reticulata section, so called because of the reticulated or netted outer coat of the bulb. They look best planted in groups in the rock garden, for they are small and are better cared for and seen in that way. The commonest species, I. reticulata, can be found in American bulb catalogs, as it is used as a greenhouse pot plant in colder climates. It is sometimes subject to a bulb disease which is at present incurable, but it is well worth planting on a small scale for the sake of its lovely deep violet-purple flowers, which have an appropriate violet scent. All the irises of this group like a well-drained soil and an open sunny spot.

For most gardens and for cut flowers, it is the members of the Xiphium group and their hybrids which are important. Because I. xiphium came from Spain, the earlier garden forms naturally were called Spanish iris. Years ago I grew them in quantity, the little bulbs being very cheap and of easy culture when planted about three inches deep in any sunny place and given drainage. In May they rewarded us with a gay show of their slender flowers—two in succession in each head—borne at the top of rather thin and inadequately foliaged stems; they are easily replaced if it is desirable to cut them to the ground, or else the scanty foliage can be left, but shortened to effect ripening of the bulb, and the whole planting covered with a shallow-rooting summer annual. The colors included white, yellow, blue, bronze, brown, and many combinations of these, such as yellow and white and blue.

These older Spanish irises have now been largely replaced by similar but taller and stronger hybrids with bigger flowers, which in California open outdoors in March or April rather than in May, and in general precede the tall bearded irises. The newer ones are called Dutch iris because they were bred in Holland, but they too are of Spanish and North African parentage and so are equally adapted to our conditions. At first they were limited to blues, but the color range is being widened to include most of the combinations of the old Spanish irises. Since improvements continue, it is best not to recommend particular varieties which may soon be superseded, but I would certainly grow Wedgewood—which presumably is derived partly from the early African Iris tingitana—for it is much earlier than most of the Dutch irises and is sturdy and persistent here, with large flowers of a lovely blue. A sunny aspect, any good garden soil with good drainage—for they do not like to get waterlogged—and a place where they can dry off in their rest period are the simple requirements, and all are easy to meet in California. My only losses came from mosaic, a virus disease which stripes the foliage and weakens the plant; there is as yet no cure for it so to prevent its being spread to others by aphis, I recommend the usual procedure of digging up and discarding occasional plants showing evidence of it.

Because English irises—a misnomer as they originally also came from Spain and Portugal, though Dutch bulb growers who got them from British importers thought they were English plants—are often offered by Pacific coast bulb dealers, my experience with them may interest other California adventurers. They are forms of Iris xiphoides and come in white, lavender, blue, and red purples, too often marred by flakings of a darker color. These dark markings may possibly be due to a virus disease—similar to the one which causes breaking of tulips—and apparently not affecting growth. The English irises are early June bloomers, and the flowers are very nice for cutting, with broad flower segments and rich colors. It has been said that no garden grows with equal success both the Spanish (or Dutch) and the English irises, dry conditions favoring the former and moisture being essential to the latter. This opinion has certainly been verified in my garden, for even when the English irises had some shade and water they were never really happy or vigorous here; they flowered indifferently when the bulbs were new, and not at all thereafter. Doubtless there are cool foggy California gardens with natural subirrigation where they are worth growing, but most of us had better leave them to gardeners in the Pacific northwest, where, around Puget Sound or Vancouver, B. C., they get what they want. The explanation of their preferences is merely that English irises like what they have been used to and their ancestors came from the pastures of the Pyrenees where, as W. R. Dykes says, "there is always moisture beneath the surface of the soil."

CHAPTER TEN

CHRYSANTHEMUMS, GERANIUMS, FUCHSIAS

———————

HESE three plants—chrysanthemums, geraniums, and fuchsias—have been selected for special attention because they are such large contributors to the beauty of California gardens. I have been much concerned at various times with the intensive cultivation of all of them, partly because they are so happy here. Where I began gardening, chrysanthemums were rarely tried outdoors because killing frosts came so early, while geraniums and fuchsias, the first plants I remember as a child, were grown only in pots or set out in beds for the summer. In Montreal, where I was born, the French Canadian women would hawk them from door to door in late May, trading them for old clothes. I can still remember my father sadly searching for a cherished pair of old pants which had been exchanged for a red geranium; my mother was a wise woman and knew the value of silence on such occasions.

CHRYSANTHEMUMS

All the chrysanthemums are hardy here, not merely the early Korean hybrids or the tough later pompons, but even the great shaggy mops grown to a single head for large decorations. The plants are hardy, but for perfection and finish the large-flowered chrysanthemums are commonly grown commercially under muslin or tiffany, sometimes even under glass. It is, however, the singles, pompons, anemones, and the decorative and spidery varieties rather than the big show chrysanthemums which are of value for garden and also for house decoration.

Chrysanthemums are heavy feeders. For good results the soil should be prepared by digging well in advance of planting out and by incorporating animal manure and a sprinkling of superphosphate. New varieties will be bought in small pots from dealers in April or early May, but older varieties in the garden will be renewed annually by cuttings of short vigorous shoots from the outside of old clumps. Three or four inches long, cut below a joint or node and with the lower leaves removed, they can be put into a glass-covered frame or box of sharp sand, shaded, and watered frequently but not too heavily. In about a month, from the bases of the cuttings several white roots will appear. The plants may then either be potted up in small pots of prepared soil, sand, leaf mold, and manure, or they may be set out closely in prepared protected beds to harden and develop. By May those in pots should have been repotted a couple of times, while those in nursery beds should have been planted out where they will flower. Select an open sunny place and give them regular thorough watering. For further fertilizing, mulch with animal manure, or rake in lightly and water in any good complete commercial fertilizer so that the growth and the leaves will be green and succulent. If bushes, mainly for garden effect, are desired this use should be kept in mind in the selection of varieties and in pinching out the tops to further branching and bush form. If the object is large cut flowers, singly on long stems, growth must be limited to a very few strong stems, and these must be kept erect by early staking or tying to wires carried on posts at each end of the row. This is, however, a commercial practice for cut flowers, not for the home garden. For prize or exhibition flowers, disbudding is necessary, but I am thinking only of general garden culture here. Pinching of garden plants should cease about July 1, but plants should be further fertilized as buds begin to appear. Spraying for aphis or thrips and for rust and mildew should be done where necessary, using a nicotine solution for the pests and a copper fungicide for the diseases.

If you are a casual or too busy gardener, you can get fair chrysanthemums, particularly of the smaller-flowered kinds, by simply pulling off each spring from the old clumps single vigorous outer shoots which have roots, topping them to reduce evaporation and induce branching, and planting them out where they will flower; if the soil is fairly rich and they are watered, they will give pretty good returns for even this culture.

No selection of varieties is given as this depends on taste, and in any case, new and improved ones are always appearing. However, I do advise against the early varieties, such as the Koreans, which flower in most California gardens while it is too warm. It is better to wait for varieties which bloom from mid-October to Thanksgiving, and for garden purposes there are many singles, pompons, anemones, small decoratives, and other forms which will provide variety and color during this time. Most people prefer the bronzes, reds, and golds as more appropriate to autumn, so it is well to let these predominate and not mix them with pale or rosy pinks in your plantings or arrangements.

GERANIUMS

The South African geraniums—botanically they are pelargoniums—are about the most valuable summer flowering plants for California, either in pots or in the open ground, where they may be treated like hardy perennials in gardens getting only a few degrees of winter frost. Under this name come the zonal geraniums with zones of a darker color on their round leaves and with big heads of single or double flowers, the ivy-leaved geraniums, mainly trailers, and what are popularly called pelargoniums or Martha Washington geraniums, with lovely flowers of a wonderful range of color, supplemented by attractive, generally contrasting markings.

The zonal geraniums are the toughest members of the family and can endure drought and neglect, but they are so much finer under favorable culture that they are worth a little attention. In the open ground they are more vigorous than in pots and sometimes grow into huge wide bushes or tall ones halfway up the side of a house. They have no special requirements, just a good garden soil, full or partial sunshine, and watering, especially when it is warm. They may be pruned, preferably in fall or winter, to shape them and keep them within bounds. The singles have the advantage of dropping their florets when they fade, while doubles often retain them. The only problem in their garden use is the clash of colors, the difficulty of finding anything to agree with some of the reds. Selection of varieties is best made when plants can be seen in bloom. I like Crabbe, salmon pink; Hall Caine, soft red; Nuit Poitvine, crimson; Maxime Kovalesky, almost orange; and Gertrude Pearson, rosy pink, but there are new ones coming on which will widen and soften the color range and give us varieties with contrasting eyes or centers.

These geraniums come easily from cuttings, preferably not too large or lush, but short-jointed pieces of about four inches, cut just below a pair of leaves and with the lower foliage removed before planting them an inch deep, either in pure sand or in a mixture of sand, fibrous loam, and leaf mold. Because they are so succulent it is much better not to put them in as soon as cut, but to leave the cuttings lying around for a day or so to dry; after drying they are less liable to rot.

For pot culture, to which they are so well adapted, start the rooted cuttings in small pots of a good mixture such as one gets from a compost heap; a fibrous loam is the general idea, and keep moving the plants to successively larger pots as they increase in size. They enjoy summer watering, every day if their location and the season are warm, and they will do well in full sun, but if they can be given some shade when they come into flower, the blooms will last longer.

Ivy geraniums, varieties of Pelargonium peltatum, have a quite different use in our gardens where their permanent green polished leaves fit them for ground covers, particularly on sunny slopes and for hanging down over retaining walls. For both purposes the old rose Charles Turner is freely used. They can also be trained upright on wire fences to give the effect of a hedge and are often found as casual climbers over outhouses and into trees, even mixed with climbing roses for later bloom. The prevalence of the double pink might suggest that pink is the only color, but there are reds and whites and lavenders, singles and doubles, and some varieties with very pleasing markings. These ivy geraniums are of the easiest culture in the open and can be grown somewhat less effectively in pots like the zonal geraniums. They merit more attention than they get and above all are plants for the busy gardener.

Pelargoniums, Martha Washington geraniums, have a greater individual claim so they have become specialists' and collectors' plants, and many lovely combinations of color have been developed to meet a demand for something new in shades or markings. As exhibition plants or for patio decoration they are best grown in pots where their individuality can be noted. Their culture in containers and in the open ground, to which they are also well adapted, is much like that of the zonal geraniums, but varieties seem to vary somewhat in vigor. In the open ground they are at their best in the sandy soil and salty air of seashore gardens. Wherever they are used in masses they are most effective, particularly in the first half of the summer, for their season of full flower does not extend to the length of the zonals.

A book could be written about these and other geraniums, including those with different scented leaves. Indeed such a book appeared in 1946 in Helen Van Pelt Wilson's *Geraniums for Windows and Gardens*. As the author made some study of California conditions before writing it, I can recommend it for required reading to those interested in this great plant family.

FUCHSIAS

Fuchsias undoubtedly are by far the finest summer-flowering shrubs for California gardens along the cool coast from San Diego to Crescent City. Even inland many can be successfully grown if special attention is given to the selection of frost-hardy and heat-resistant varieties and to local requirements of culture. That most fuchsias are hardy enough here to stand half a dozen degrees of frost and in the open ground to develop into huge shrubs and live to great age is a matter of astonishment to those who have always thought of them as summer bedding or pot plants. Yet their toughness is shown by their persistence in old gardens through the first third of this century, during which they were quite neglected for no reason other than fashion in flowers. With the founding of the American Fuchsia Society in Berkeley in 1929 came a wonderful revival of interest and the development of a fuchsia cult which is entirely justified. Though I participated actively in its earlier work and was able to select in England and import many of the new fuchsias, which have since been used by California breeders, I shall treat the fuchsia here not as a specialist's flower to be collected and grown to perfection, but as a shrub of peculiar adaptability to our conditions.

The garden fuchsias which have been raised in the last hundred years are hybrids, now so mixed that though some of their wild parents came from as far north as Mexico, from upland American tropics, or from colder southern Chile, they have certain general characteristics. Outdoors they are summer flowering and revel in cool foggy coastal conditions and in moisture, which of course must be furnished them in California summers. The degree of shade to be given them depends on the local sunshine and fog, but in general it may be said that they prefer eastern exposures where only morning sunshine comes. They particularly dislike hot afternoon sunshine and warm drying winds and are at their best in filtered sunshine such as they would get in a lath house or on the east side of a wall or fence, solid below and latticed above. Drainage is also very necessary, for though they love summer moisture they can be drowned out by the presence of stagnant water around the roots. They are hearty feeders, and while indifferent to particular soils, they have to make such a vigorous vegetative spring growth to produce many fine flowers that moisture-retaining humus and food in the form of animal manure are highly desirable; fish meal, cottonseed meal, or chemical fertilizers may have a supplementary use. Thorough preparation of the soil is particularly desirable if fuchsias are to be allowed to remain long in one place and develop into large shrubs. Mulches of old manure, peat, or other humus which will keep the roots cool in summer are recommended. Fuchsias require no cultivation of the soil and in summer would in fact be injured by it as their roots are often near the surface.

Summer moisture both at the roots and in the air is essential for great success. While the soil should be kept damp by thorough soakings, a fine spray which will give what one of our finest growers calls a halo of humidity all around the plants is also highly desirable.

New fuchsia plantings are wisely made in early spring as soon as danger of frost is over and young greenhouse-grown plants are available. Varieties differ so greatly in vigor, in size, or in character of growth, that specific planting distances cannot be recommended. Unless varieties known to be dwarf and bushy are being set out, it is well to provide at the beginning a stake to hold up the plant and to give the often necessary backbone for its future framework. Spring is the time of strong vegetative growth, and no flowers should be expected or wanted until early summer. Hand pinching of the young shoots is the best method of training the plant in the way it should grow. After summer sets in, flowers come, continuously in some varieties but in successive crops with others, until with the lessening daylight of autumn plants go into their period of decline for the year. It is futile to try by feeding or watering to keep up flowering outdoors through the winter, though some few varieties will do this naturally in a warm rainy season.

In established plantings, heavy pruning should be done during the dormant period, preferably in early spring when danger of frost is past. Indeed such pruning is essential to stimulate that new growth which alone produces summer flowers. Weak branches of no value should be entirely removed, and those retained cut back hard even to the point of leaving only two or three pairs of dormant buds. Old bushes will stand very drastic treatment if that is necessary to keep them in bounds. Summer pruning should be limited to the removal of unwanted branches and whatever pinching back is desirable for training.

Commercial propagation is altogether under glass in winter and from tip cuttings of new growth; these naturally give larger and better plants earlier in the season. Amateurs may increase their plants in spring by similar cuttings taken from the current growth which is severed just below a node, the lower leaves removed, and the cuttings inserted a third of their length in damp sand. Kept moist under a bell glass, they will root well but require attention. Cuttings from better ripened wood of the same season, taken preferably with a heel, the growing tips removed, the pieces put in a sandbox—about an inch is imbedded—and kept moist by syringing, root readily in summer and need less care than soft green tips. Still less trouble are hardwood cuttings. These are merely large pieces, preferably of unbloomed ripened wood, put half their length in a sandy bed or trench in autumn; they need no care but of course take several months to root and do not give as fine plants as the other methods.

VARIETIES OF FUCHSIAS

Selection of varieties will depend largely on the purpose for which fuchsias are being planted and sometimes on climatic conditions. The hardiest and most vigorous ones are F. magellanica (F. macrostemma) and its forms, such as the slender gracilis and the tough and drought-resistant but colorful Ric-

184

cartonii, which might well be more used in California for informal hedges. All these have relatively small red and blue single flowers, as have a number of somewhat larger hybrids. There are similar red and white ones like Mme. Cornelissen, strong upright growers which thrive under adverse conditions. Other old varieties which I have found will stand adversity are Rose of Castile, white and red purple; Schiller; Mme. Thibaud, with wonderful terminal clusters of rose and purple; the tall and vigorous Daniel Lambert; Display, with wide open rosy flowers; and Marinka, a fine pendulant red which grown against a wall reaches as far as the second story. These represent the sturdy old peasantry of the family, but recently some hybrids of Fuchsia lycioides, nice bush plants—Esperanza, Mephisto, Mademoiselle, and Pastel are examples—have been added to this class. There are also some good medium or dwarf husky growers, like the salmon-coral Sunset or the purple and scarlet Lord Byron, which are the best choice where sturdy, floriferous, upright, but compact specimens or groups are needed.

Among the doubles, better used as specimens, are such good bourgeois fuchsias as Suzanne Pasquier and Flocon de Neige, quite different red and whites; Fascination; Gypsy Queen, mauve and red; Phenomenal, red and purple; and Beauty of Exeter, a red self. They demand more care and food and drink but are not temperamental. Among the fine ladies, requiring more attention but rewarding the giver in perfection of flowers, are certain singles like Lucienne Breval, The Doctor, Gay Senorita, Melody, and Aurora Superba and its orange relatives, and among the doubles, the pale pink and whites of which Patty Evans (better than Rolla) and Ave Maria are good examples. Some very desirable ones are trailing in habit, like Cascade and its sisters, Mrs. Rundle, or Nonpareil, or among newer ones, Victory and Wistaria; these call for special attention to staking and pruning, or growing to large heads on standard stems. They are obviously better as specimens than for grouping or landscape work. In addition there is a group of triphylla hybrids, far more susceptible to frosts than most fuchsias but cheerfully taking more heat and sun. They have longer tubes and flowers generally of orange red like Gartenmeister Bonstedt or rosy salmon like Leverkusen.

For the specialist there are several species and also hundreds of new garden seedlings being raised by California breeders, but the cult of the fuchsia can hardly be discussed here. The publications of the American Fuchsia Society, including The Fuchsia Book, are required reading for addicts, as are the catalogs of specialists.

FUCHSIAS IN POTS

Fuchsias grown in pots may be the answer for those without proper garden conditions. In pots they may be placed for more intimate association on shaded patios, in arbors, or lath houses. Here culture must be intensive, the young plants started in smaller pots of rich soil mixture, as they grow shifted into larger pots, shaped by pinching, fed by liquid or artificial manures, and regularly watered. Glazed pots are now generally considered preferable to unglazed ones since they are more retentive of moisture. Glazed clay hanging baskets or containers made of redwood are excellent receptacles for the many lovely trailing varieties which are best grown in that way. For quick results it is a good plan to start three plants of the same variety in a pot rather than one.

CHAPTER ELEVEN

SPRING-FLOWERING BULBS

———

*G*RANTED that the California gardener does not get the thrill of seeing the earliest bulbs come through the snow and never experiences fully the sense of nature waking from sleep, he has compensations. His spring really begins with the late autumn rains and continues until they slow down or cease in April. His spring is not only prolonged so that all spring bulbs flower over a much longer period, but he has to contend with neither snow nor ice. Moreover he can grow many spring bulbs which are not hardy outdoors in much of the United States, in particular some from South Africa and others from the Mediterranean.

SNOWFLAKES AND SNOWDROPS

The snowflakes usher in the season, beginning in December and flowering in one form or other for three months or more. Though generally referred to as the spring snowflake, Leucojum vernum, the species found in California gardens—in spite of when it flowers here—is certainly the summer snowflake, Leucojum aestivum, a much taller, stronger species with several rather than single flowers. It has strap-shaped leaves, twelve to eighteen inches long, and flower stems as high or higher, with from three to five dainty hanging white flowers, each of the six equal parts being tipped with green. Planted in autumn about four inches deep, either in sun or partial shade, and left undisturbed for years, it comes up cheerfully each season. The type with smaller flowers is the earliest here and the common one everywhere, but I have a few bulbs of later, larger, more expensive forms with bigger bells on taller stems, and these can sometimes be found under the name Gravetye variety. The typical form is inexpensive enough to naturalize, and in California does better than any other bulb I know so treated; it not only grows freely, but it looks wild, quite lacking the bourgeois well-fed appearance of most Dutch bulbs.

Snowdrops, which are often the first flowers of spring in cold climates, are infrequently seen in California gardens. In my experience the common snowdrop, Galanthus nivalis, grown in eastern America, cannot endure our warm winters or long dry summers and is not worth trying in coastal California, but the giant snowdrop, Galanthus Elwesii, from warmer Asia Minor, does very well. As I write this in mid-January, many flowers are open in a clump planted in a cool location some years ago. Apparently the snowdrops are best left undisturbed. From a little tuft of broad gray-green leaves about four inches high comes a stem holding above them a single flower with three flaring pure white outer segments and short inner ones tipped green—a wholly delightful thing. I plan to get more of these inexpensive bulbs to plant in cool places and in clumps easy to find rather than as singles. Group planting is best with all small bulbs, I think.

CROCUSES

In the east, crocuses, heralding spring as they come through the snow, have little competition for attention. In California, they are noticeable only for their modesty and their sentiment.

After trials of the relatively obese Dutch garden crocuses, I have given up growing them, as they are comparatively late and also short-lived. But certain early spring-flowering species planted many years ago continue to come up every January and have apparently naturalized—that is perpetuated themselves by seed—where they have found themselves undisturbed in the partial shade of deciduous shrubs, fuchsias in this case, or shrublets, thyme in one instance. As they are inexpensive, they are worth a trial, and our bulb dealers should stock them. Crocus Sieberi, a Grecian species, is first to bloom here with light lilac flowers, and C. tomasinianus from Dalmatia follows it with somewhat similar coloring though a little bluer. Among deep yellows, Crocus moesicus (C. aureus) is the most persistent I have grown and blooms in January, as does C. biflorus, a striped blue and white. Perhaps our big lazy orange cat, Naranja, is entitled to some credit for the permanence of these lovely little things, for mice are fond of them and Naranja is fond of mice. I am hoping now I can get more of these spring species like the lilac and buff C. Imperati, which come from Italy and are therefore likely to do well in our comparable climate. They require no special culture, just plant a patch of the small corms about three inches deep and a little farther apart, and leave them undisturbed.

STAR-FLOWERS

About the most indestructible little bulb we grow is the spring star-flower, which has been variously named by botanists Brodiaea uniflora, Triteleia uniflora, Milla uniflora, and Leucocoryne uniflora. Bailey's *Hortus II* favors the first, but bulb catalogs are more likely to use the second. In spite of such a load of names this little Argentinian member of the garlic family—with leaves to taste—persists under all conditions, even when its little white bulbs are dug under, and constantly increases. Above its almost flat foliage appear in very early spring innumerable single white star-shaped flowers two or three inches high; sometimes they have quite a bluish tinge. No special culture is necessary. I have never known star-flowers to fail. Here they carpet areas under or among bigger things, and some are even encroaching on the paths. They are never a nuisance, but not good for picking unless you like garlic in more places than salad.

GRAPE HYACINTHS

The Muscari, or grape hyacinths, are perhaps more effective than most minor bulbs in the early spring garden, where patches of blue on the ground under pink-flowering fruit trees can be very lovely. The bulbs are inexpensive and of the easiest culture, doing a bit better for me in semishade than in full sunshine. They are also much more effective when they are well enough established for the bulbs to produce strong colorful masses of urnlike flowers. The common grape hyacinth, Muscari botryoides, has leaves about a foot long and good deep blue flowers. The variety Heavenly Blue, in spite of its nice name, I found inferior to Muscari armeniacum, which has shorter foliage and a neater habit after flowering. There is a dainty little white form of M. botryoides which in my garden hardly increases at all but persists unmoved for many years. Plant it close as all these bulbs are so much better in masses. Years ago I imported from Holland under the name Muscari azureum— now called Hyacinthus ciliatus by Bailey, and formerly H. azureus—what to simple gardeners like myself seemed just a beautiful Alice-blue grape hyacinth. It was a relatively weak grower and diminished rather than increased, but its color was so clear and clean I would like to try it again.

BLUEBELLS

The bulbous bluebells, squills, or scillas, certainly justify far more general use in our spring gardens than they have had. Perhaps the reason for their relative neglect has been that until recent years the species best adapted to our needs has not been widely known. Gardeners from the eastern United States, where the Siberian squill, Scilla sibirica, is widely planted for carpets or patches of lovely, almost ground-level blue, are disappointed to find that it is worthless here. I have tried it and could hardly get any flowers even the first year. After all, why should Siberian plants like California? We don't try to acclimatize Eskimos. English gardeners think of the bluebells in May at Kew Gardens, where they carpet the ground under deciduous trees and often make it bluer than the English skies. This is the English bluebell, Scilla nonscripta, formerly called Scilla nutans, a native of the British Isles, as naturally happy there as in similar climates like that of the Pacific Northwest. I have grown it here, and in a cool watered place it got by and remained some years, but that was not good enough.

In California we can do better, for there is a Spanish bluebell, a species, Scilla hispanica (still almost universally called Scilla campanulata in bulb books and in catalogs), which, coming from a climate much like that of California, is perfectly happy here, is indestructible, and increases rapidly. Not unlike a larger English bluebell, it is a more vigorous grower with larger leafage, taller stems—over a foot high in some forms— which are more upright than those of the English bluebells. If the bulbs are planted about four inches deep and as far apart, preferably in half shade—for blue shows up best there—they can be left alone for years. Meantime they will have filled up intervening spaces with bulbs to produce a solid sheet of blue which remains for some weeks, since there are a number of flowers on each stem. In our garden we have used this scilla in various ways, but the largest and most effective plantings appear as spring ground cover to our apple trees. After the blue-bell foliage dies down in early summer, it is hoed off and the ground left bare and dry. My first choice of all these bluebells is the giant variety Excelsior, a tall, vigorous, and prolific blue form now generally available on the Pacific Coast. There are white varieties of S. hispanica, nice for certain purposes, and also what the catalogs, under such names as Peach Blossom and Rose Queen, optimistically call pinks. I have tried several, but they are all rather disappointing, none of them clear or brilliant.

DUTCH HYACINTHS

Dutch hyacinths meant very little in my early garden life. Perhaps I had never seen them growing in anything but formal Victorian bedding, where a certain uncompromising rigid uprightness and a middle-aged stodgy form combined to leave me uninterested. Though I have become more charitable, hyacinth breeders still seem to me to have shown little imagination; flowers really need to be more than just substantial. Had I a few more lives I might possibly devote one to crashing all the Dutch ideals and try to raise a race of hyacinths with the lightness and grace of youth. There exists one such, the rather infrequently seen Oranje Boven, "orange-salmon, loosely arranged, very elegant spikes (small bulb)"—I quote from Van Tubergen's catalog—and it is my favorite of all Dutch hyacinths.

In spite of the fact that they never can be wild or natural and fit perfectly into our kind of garden, I find Dutch hyacinths so early and so desirable for their fragrance and range of colors —nothing else in their season gives such a series of pink, rose, red, blue, and purple—that we now grow a considerable number and variety. Some varieties have died out, but others, either more vigorous or happy in their conditions, have persisted; some have increased into clumps, and seedlings have even appeared in one old planting. Formerly our hyacinths were planted in groups, each of a single variety, as I had bought a collection of named varieties; now they are scattered to produce a Dresden-china effect under our apple trees. Particularly where they are to be planted informally and left several years, I prefer, for more than reasons of economy, to buy the smallest size bulbs which are sometimes called miniatures or cynthella hyacinths. Their spikes will be smaller, and they will take longer to produce those large blooms which seem to me too heavy. They are also apt to fall over in downpours such as often occur in their flowering season. We have given them no special culture, just planted them in regular soil about five inches deep and rather more apart, and left them alone. They are undeniably colorful and deliciously fragrant in spring, and visitors seem ready to admire them for these virtues alone. I give no selection of varieties, though personally I like clear pinks and pale blues best. With doubles I will have no concern.

DAFFODILS

Daffodils are the most grown and featured of spring bulbs in our garden. Almost entirely across it, down east of the house, runs a double daffodil border about one hundred and fifty feet long with varying depths on each side. Shrubs screen it from above and give background to the west, and a few brooms have been planted below the lower side to afford variation and suggest a boundary there. I have long been devoted to daffodils and irises so they have been given prominence in our gardens. Like a sailor's loves in different ports, they are not in conflict for my attention, though it is time and season which separates them, rather than space. It will therefore be hard for me to give them only a due proportion of this chapter. I could write a book about them, and if I live long enough I think I will.

It is easy to defend the choice of the daffodil—using the good old English name for the whole narcissus family—as the greatest spring-flowering bulb. Not only is it early, for Narcissus Paper White can be brought into bloom in California before Christmas, but by a selection of varieties we can have daffodils for months, with the main show in February and March. More than any other spring-flowering bulb does the daffodil have that range of form, those fine variations of color—in an admittedly limited range—and the individuality which endear it to its adherents. Further, there are daffodils for many purposes, dainty little things for the rock garden, big flaunting yellow trumpets for mass plantings, and late flat-flowered Barriis for beauty of individual flower. Finally, daffodils are without competitors in their season as cut flowers, lasting for days in cool rooms.

Daffodils, in spite of considerable losses through diseases and pests—for which there are as yet no adequate controls—are still by far the most permanent of the major spring bulbs. From one danger of California gardens, the pocket gopher, they are free, for while these rodents greedily gorge on tulips and many other bulbs, nature has provided the members of the Narcissus family with an acrid taste, due to some poisonous substance, which is a perfect repellent. Many of the older varieties have persisted with us for years, uncared-for and undisturbed, until final overcrowding has reduced their flowering, as is natural in slum conditions. It is a great asset to have some bulbs which do not need continual replanting, and though doubtless the finer forms are best lifted every couple of years, this is not essential. As a last argument, they are of the easiest culture, easily weeded, watered almost wholly by our winter rains, and adapted to a wide range of soils and situations.

Suggestions for growing daffodils seem in order since our California conditions are in some respects peculiar. The Narcissus family, the wild parents of our garden daffodils, come from areas north of the Mediterranean. The bunch-flowered polyanthus or tazetta species are from the warmer, drier coasts, but the trumpets and Poets narcissus—progenitors of our many garden hybrids—are from higher up, from the Alps or Pyrenees, where they get a winter sleep, lots of water when growing and flowering, and a much shorter period of rest than the long dry summers here naturally enforce. Therefore places like Ireland, coastal Oregon, Washington, and British Columbia, which are characterized by long wet springs and shorter, cooler summers, have provided the best garden conditions for the daffodils' high-bred garden descendants. This must be kept in mind in selecting situations for daffodils, for if one has a choice, it is better in California to select cooler rather than warmer places and eastern or northern slopes or exposures rather than areas toward the west. It should also be remembered that daffodils tend to face the sun and that they are therefore best planted north or east of a path so that they will look toward it rather than turn to it their less attractive backs.

On a large scale, daffodils are best in borders or separated areas not too near the house, so that they can be forgotten when their foliage is drying down or the ground is quite bare. The necessity of letting the foliage dry off naturally—if flowers are to be expected next season—makes them a liability in too prominent places, as for example along the base of the house. They never look well in long thin rows, so if only a few are planted let them be in groups. Where they are included in the herbaceous border they leave blanks when out of flower, although they may be interplanted with Dutch irises for later flowers, and covered with annuals like petunias, nasturtiums, or other sprawling shallow-rooting subjects for summer. The water they will get in such places will do them no harm. In spite of the wide belief of California gardeners that daffodils resent water, this is not so. They really prefer a shorter dry season than ours and so do well in places where the summer rain cannot be kept off them.

If I could order my soil, I would ask for a rich sandy loam such as one finds around Santa Cruz. It is easier to work, gives cleaner bulbs, and they seem less subject to basal rot when the soil is lighter and the drainage better. On the other hand, in our heavier black soil they grow taller and produce larger flowers. If the soil is very heavy or gets waterlogged, I would put a good handful of sand directly under very fine or expensive bulbs as a deterrent to basal rot. Poor hungry soils should be enriched, and it is doubtful if there is anything better than a mixture of bone meal and bone flour dug into the ground below the point where bulbs rest. I have used no surface fertilizers. Digging the soil a couple of feet deep is ideal preparation, but more than I can afford; I might do it if I had fewer bulbs—mine, like children in large families, get on without too much coddling.

Daffodil bulbs do not have as long a period of inactivity as most bulbs; if left in ground which gets even moderately damp, they resume root growth by September. It is therefore better to plant early, in September or October, than late, though long after Christmas I have planted bulbs which were given to me; this saved the bulbs but gave poor late flowers that season. The rule for depth of planting is that the base of the bulb should be five inches below the surface of the soil, but nothing terrible happens if there is variation. We lift novelties every second year, that is, after the second season down, but this is to inspect the bulbs and divide them for quicker increase. Less valuable varieties are left sometimes for five years or more till they show crowding and deterioration; there is no rule about this. Digging is done in August, and the ideal is immediate replanting, but the bulbs often remain in flats in the shade or in the basement for a month or more although never in heat or sun. We plant rather casually, placing big bulbs six or eight inches apart, but varieties with smaller ones considerably closer. Wire stakes with as permanent labels as are obtainable are desirable for marking, but a paper plan of any extensive planting is also essential.

We usually water after planting, to get the bulbs growing and even to start the weeds. It has been our experience that if we can get a good germination of weeds before the heavy rains, we can hoe them off before the daffodils come up, and no more weeding will be required until the foliage dies down. Watering during the growing season is necessary only in dry winters or in very warm situations. When we get a January or February drought we soak the beds. I agree with the late Carl Purdy that daffodils never get too much water when in growth; they love it, and water increases size of flower and length of stem.

PEST AND DISEASE

The pest which is responsible for the greatest loss of bulbs is the daffodil fly, fortunately not nearly as common in California as farther north. It usually appears toward the end of the flowering season and lays eggs at the base of the foliage. As the ground shrinks around the stem, the eggs drop down onto the bulbs where they develop by midsummer into fat unpleasant grubs, which eat out the whole center of the bulb and as a rule destroy it. Frequent lifting and destruction of infested bulbs—easily spotted by their soft necks—will reduce infestation; perhaps mulching the ground around the stems will also help. Specific deterrents like naphthalene flakes have some followers, but a really effective control is not now available; perhaps DDT may be the answer. In my garden, nematodes, which are most destructive in England, have not been very evident, probably because commercial growers have got them under control by the hot water treatment, which involves soaking dormant bulbs for three to five hours at 110 to 112 degrees. Basal rot has hit us badly at times. Formerly we dusted with ceresan, but lately, before replanting, we have substituted the dipping of all bulbs for some minutes in a bucket of water containing a three per cent formaldehyde solution; this seems more effective. Yellow stripe (mosaic) is a virus disease and incurable as yet; growers simply discard plants with infected foliage.

A long season of bloom and a wide range of form and color are dependent on a careful selection of varieties. There are rather elaborate classifications of daffodils, but for the average amateur these, with their largely obsolete terminology, can be disregarded. The first selection which follows comprises only inexpensive varieties—generally found in American bulb catalogs—and it contains representatives of all groups.

INEXPENSIVE DAFFODILS

Paper White and Soleil d'Or are the best of the early bunch-flowered tazettas or polyanthus. Both are better than the related Chinese Sacred Lily, a narcissus despite its name. Among true daffodils, with a single flower to a stem, King Alfred, which is early and deep yellow, and Aerolite, late and a pale yellow, are fine trumpets; a good yellow and white bicolor trumpet, is Spring Glory; Mme. Krelage is the best near-white inexpensive trumpet.

Coming to those which have cups rather than trumpets, really better garden plants, as they are less likely to be top-heavy and so fall on their faces, I pick Carlton and Lucinius as about the earliest and the latest of all yellow incomparabilis or large cup varieties. There are as yet no cheap very good yellows with red cups, but Helios is an approach, as its cup is orange, and Bath's Flame is a big improvement over old Barrii Conspicuous. Among daffodils with white perianths and large yellow cups, Silver Star is fine and early, John Evelyn later and distinct, and Diana Kasner quite late, while of those with short, nearly flat cups I would select Firetail, a fine contrast of white perianth and red cup, Nette O'Melveny with pale yellow cup, and Hera nearly pure white, all late. Among the flat Poets narcissus I give first choice to Actaea for its size, vigor, and general dependability here. From the crosses made between poets and tazettas, a group now called poetaz, you can make no mistake with Laurens Koster, white, and Klondyke, yellow perianthed, varieties.

Among distinctive smaller things, I should not want to be

without the very early cyclamineus hybrid February Gold. The old natural hybrid Campernelle Jonquil is very vigorous and reliable. Golden Sceptre would be most people's choice of larger jonquil hybrids. From Narcissus triandrus crossed with garden daffodils there have been raised many lovely, somewhat nodding, white hybrids of which the now inexpensive Moonshine and Thalia are good examples; these are very late. I don't care for doubles, as form seems so important in daffodils, but if they are wanted for cutting, there are the dainty sweet-scented Jonquilla flore pleno, the double poetaz Cheerfulness, and the larger Twink, of mixed primrose and orange petals, all quite distinct.

FINER VARIETIES

As you develop interest and begin to want the finer daffodils, consider adding the huge early yellow trumpet Diotima, the big white trumpet Beersheba (but only if you have a cold garden), the startling pink trumpet Mrs. R. O. Backhouse, Fortune, a yellow with a deeper cup, Tunis, a white with a yellow cup bronze-rimmed (these last two being among the earliest and most improved); and perhaps also Daisy Schaffer, St. Egwin, Hades, and Silver Chimes, which is a triandrus-tazetta cross.

Advances in daffodils will be great, but as the novelty varieties increase slowly, most of the better ones will remain expensive and likely to be found for some time only in the collections of specialists and breeders. My selection includes among yellow trumpets, St. Issey and Galway; white trumpets, Cameronian and Broughshane; somewhat buff and pink, Trousseau and Carnlough; yellows with red cups, Carbineer, Porthilly, Diolite, but even these will soon be superseded; white with yellow cup, Polindra; whites with red cups, Jean Hood, early, and Coronach, late. The best novelty I have seen for years is Green Island, still so expensive as to be far beyond the reach of most of us.

For rock gardens there are several little Narcissus species, dainty and wild and in California less persistent. Our greatest success has been with N. canaliculatus, a miniature tazetta requiring a warm place to ripen its bulbs and set its flower buds; N. bulbocodium conspicuus, the yellow hoop-petticoat daffodil likes good drainage but is otherwise easy here. The related N. bulbocodium Clusii (or monophyllus) from Morocco, a tiny white, opening almost like a morning-glory, dies out—a matter of regret, for it is very early and charming. The exquisite N. triandrus, sometimes called Angel's Tears, dies out too, but it also self-sows so that there are generally a few of its flowers around.

TULIPS

Until recent years we have always grown many tulips: that they have now disappeared from our garden is an acknowledgment that they were too great an annual cost and care and, in spite of their wonderful colors, less appropriate to our informal garden than other spring-flowering bulbs. For the modern tulip, with its gorgeous cup of color, is a formal man-made flower, best planted in masses and in careful color schemes, and better suited to formal beds and borders where the bulbs can be replaced overnight by summer annuals or tender perennials. When we were in England in 1930, we made notes of the elaborate use of tulips at Hampton Court and in the London parks —yellow tulips interplanted with red wallflowers and forget-me-nots, bronze tulips with yellow wallflowers, purple tulips with white candytuft and purple aubrietias, pink tulips with the little pink daisy, Bellis perennis, and tulips of various colors underplanted with pansies for appropriate contrast. Had we returned to England in midsummer, we would have seen the tulips and spring-bedding plants replaced by petunias, snapdragons, dwarf single dahlias, or other summer-flowering plants. Treated in this way in small formal gardens—particularly those on level ground—tulips leave an unforgettable impression of glorious color, but the expense and work of annual replacement and of succession crops for them are beyond our means or time.

Again I have to acknowledge that our heavy soil and relatively poor culture are not what tulips demand. They want a fairly light soil, deeply dug, and well fertilized underneath, and the flowers will last longer in California if they get more morning than afternoon sun. Planted about five inches deep and perhaps a little farther apart, they are quite happy and effective in many gardens. It is one of their advantages that tulips may be planted rather late in autumn and still do very well in California where root growth can go on all winter; I have even bought bargain bulbs in January and had good success with the more vigorous varieties, though they are better in the ground by Thanksgiving. It has not been my own experience or observation here that tulips can ever be depended on to give a second year the grand show they put on the first year from the large mature bulbs sent out by growers. These are carefully selected to be just ready for fine flowering, and they have a great tendency after blooming to break up into a number of smaller bulbs, few or none of which will flower again until they have been grown on in a nursery to larger size—a slow, labor- and space-consuming practice hardly worth following. It is better to grow fewer tulips and to replace them yearly with new bulbs, a plan which, if costly, at least allows one to dig or pull up the tulips and discard them just as soon as they have finished flowering.

Gardening is not a subject about which to be dogmatic; whenever I get so, someone writes me that he has done successfully what I have advised against. So I had better say here that I have found that if certain tulips of more than ordinary vigor are left undug and their foliage allowed to die down naturally, they will continue to flower well and increase for some years. I planted in half shade a patch of that fine old Cottage tulip, Inglescomb Pink, let it alone, and three or four years later there were half a dozen flowers from each bulb, admittedly smaller blooms than those of the first year, but the effect in this informal planting was even better than at the beginning. The old Breeder tulip Bronze Queen also persisted fairly well under similar treatment, as have a few others, particularly the species tulips, which are generally more permanent.

I probably would again plant small colonies on the cool side of shrubbery groups, for there is really nothing to compare with tulips for glowing spring color, but in this big garden on the edge of the wild the pocket gophers are with us always, and in spite of successful trapping and the help of our cat they always find our tulip bulbs if we leave them in the ground over summer, at which time no distance seems too great for the gophers to travel for this preferred food. If our garden were smaller and in the city, I would put little clumps of tulips, a dozen or so of a variety, through the herbaceous border, carpet the ground under them with a sowing of sweet alyssum, Virginian stock, or Linaria Fairy Bouquet, and screen the patches with surrounding summer perennials, or cover the subsequently bare places with light-rooting sprawling annuals.

SELECTED TULIPS

There are so many good tulips I hesitate to recommend special varieties. For bedding, you might select the tall clear-colored Darwins for reds, roses, pinks, and whites; from the Breeders, for bronzes, browns, and lovely rich blends; and from the Cottage tulips with big rounded petals you might pick out whites, reds, pinks, and yellows—the best yellows being from this Cottage section. For more natural effects tulips like La Merveille or Picotee, with pointed or recurved petals are better, and these are found among the tulip species—a small group of Clusiana, the little Lady Tulip, in white and crimson, is something quite different from a group of well-fed burghers of the Darwin type. The early single or double tulips —once so evident in spring bedding in eastern parks and gardens—are not for us; they rarely make adequate stems for they flower too quickly in our often warm February.

MORAEAS

Irises have been given a chapter to themselves. Although there are a number of spring-flowering bulbous irises which I might now consider, I have chosen to discuss them at the end of the iris chapter. The related bulbous moraeas, however, deserve brief mention here. I have grown two of them. Moraea glaucopis, formerly called Iris pavonia, the peacock iris, is a little bulb for the rock garden or other elevated situation where its charm will not be overlooked and it will not be crowded out by more rampant things. Plant the bulbs in autumn an inch or so deep, and in spring the flowers, which are about an inch and a half across and white with basal spots of peacock blue, will appear on foot-high stems and last about three days. Moraea polystachia, a much taller, showier species bearing lilac flowers with basal orange spots, I have just begun to grow. Though by successive plantings it can be flowered over many months in southern California, I have mentioned it here as it is usually planted in fall for its main flowering season, which is winter and spring.

ANEMONES AND RANUNCULUS

The spring-flowering anemones and ranunculus, so gay and so useful for beds and borders, come not from bulbs but from tubers; however, their treatment and their season of flower justify consideration here. They have disappeared from this garden from no demerits of their own but simply because quail liked them as well as we did and kept the new growth so cropped to the ground that they never got a chance to grow or to bloom unless we protected them. Being particularly fond of ranunculus, we grew them for years under frames made with wooden sides a foot high and chicken wire tops. By the time the succulent young growth had hardened and the foliage reached the wire they had lost, like old asparagus, all attraction for the birds, and the frames were removed. As far as culture is concerned, anemones and ranunculus, both Mediterranean plants, are well adapted to California conditions and to fall planting, while in colder climates the roots have to be left in storage until the hard winter frosts are over.

The anemones offered in California are forms of Anemone coronaria and have poppylike flowers, generally single, but there is a strain, the St. Brigid, with double and semidouble blooms. The flowers have a fine fresh range of color—white, blue, rose, and crimson, but never yellow. They grow on foot-high stems above finely divided green leafage. Soak the gnarled and odd-shaped tuberous roots overnight and then plant them, rounded bottom side down, with the hairy surfaces about an inch below the ground. Place the tubers about eight inches apart for full effect. Anemones like a sunny place and a light rich soil, well dug; they were not happy in the heavy adobe of our Stanford garden. When bloom is over, it is best to dig up and discard the tubers, as they are never as good again, having been grown from seed the previous year to be just at their best when you got them. However, if you like raising things from seed or have more time than money, save a few good flowers for seed. Sow this in early summer in a frame in half shade and grow the plants on; transplant them in fall to where you want them to flower the following spring. For garden effect, anemones are best massed in beds by themselves, in separate colors if that is preferred, though they harmonize so well and are so gay and cheerful in mixture that most of us prefer them that way. There are other less showy strains of tuberous-rooted anemones with small, more starlike flowers, forms of A. hortensis and A. fulgens, which we have grown in pockets in the rock garden and which persisted several seasons, gradually dying out. It is too bad that these and also Anemone apennina from Italy and the related A. blanda from Greece are not available to California gardeners, as they are delightful little things. We shall always remember eating our lunch one day in early March on a hillside near Rome on the way to Tivoli and seeing the A. apennina in flower in the grass all around us.

Ranunculus have been so greatly improved in recent years by California breeders and growers that they are now of great value, not only for bedding in formal gardens and for cut flowers, for which purpose they are ideal, but for colorful displays in small gardens where space is valuable and they can be replaced later by summer annuals. They are lovely and rich in effect in mixed plantings of white, yellow, orange, pink, rose, and red to deepest shades, and they are also available in separate color groups. There are no blues among ranunculus. Give preference to the fully double strains; the flowers are more effective and last longer. The little tubers, grown commercially from seed sown the previous year, are inexpensive and come in several sizes, the biggest ones giving the most flowers. A light rich sandy soil seems best. The tubers should be planted, prongs down, with crowns about an inch below the surface of the soil. Do not plant before October—it is too warm—but from then on make plantings for a succession of bloom. It has been my experience, even in cool Berkeley, that ranunculus are better in seasons when we do not have hot dry winter weather, so a cool place is what I have preferred for them; when in full growth they love plenty of water. After flowering, the tubers may be discarded, but if allowed to dry off naturally they can be lifted, separated into single tubers like the ones originally planted, and put back again in autumn. Seed can also be selected from the best forms. It is sown in August and kept cool and damp. Then the little plants are set out in October, or later, for spring flowering and the making of tubers for the next year.

SOUTH AFRICANS

My acquaintance with those South African bulbs which are planted here in fall for spring flowering—ixias and sparaxis in particular—began in my first spring in California when I discovered them on the Stanford campus in the casual but always interesting garden of Professor D. H. Campbell. As they were then inexpensive and easily obtainable from Holland, I tried many in my Stanford garden and later in Berkeley. These South African irids are hardy along coastal California, and coming from a climate a good deal like ours, they are happy here outdoors, while in most other parts of the United States they are only suitable for culture under glass. They have proved less adapted to our present cool garden with its heavy soil than to the former garden facing west and having more afternoon sunshine. I am sure that they deserve wider growing in southern California. They practically all like the same conditions, a sunny place and light sandy soil, well drained. They are all sure to flower well from commercial bulbs and to increase fairly rapidly. Planted a couple of inches deep and somewhat farther apart at any time in autumn, these South Africans grow all winter and flower in spring. Then the foliage dies down and they go into summer rest. Because they prefer to be dry when dormant, they are best planted by themselves and in places where their beauty does not have to compete with gaudier things or with neighbors of lush growth. Borders or dry rock gardens in full sun are perhaps best, but most of them are tough and persistent and also do quite well in partial shade, if they are not overgrown by other plants. They are all fairly easy to raise from seed, and unlike most plants from bulbs or corms, they flower quickly, some the first, others the second year after sowing. In my garden most of them have persisted year after year without being moved or replanted, a very ingratiating characteristic when so many things demand more attention. Some self-sow and have naturalized in a mild way.

FREESIAS

Doubtless of all the South African bulbs, freesias are most commonly grown in California for early spring flowers. The kind now planted are not the originally imported species but really beautiful hybrids, some of which have been raised in Europe, and others, more recently, in California. These hybrids are taller and stronger in growth than the species and have larger flowers in a wide range of lovely colors including white, pink, rose, and red shades, yellows and oranges and lavenders and mauves. They still retain much of the original sweetness of their wild ancestors. Though they are obtainable in separate colors, I have always grown freesias in mixture, and they certainly blend together beautifully. Our garden is unfortunately a bit cold for them, and in 1932 and 1937, years of killing frosts, we lost a good many, but as they self-sow—we have never replaced them—they keep coming up casually. Many gardeners do not realize that freesia seed can be sown in flats in August, and the resultant plants moved out into the garden for flowering the next spring, when the best may be selected for increase by bulb division or the bed left as a mass. Freesias are of course even easier to grow from bulbs which are obtainable by September or October for planting soon after. They should be set about two inches deep and pointed up. In our garden the only difficulty, apart from frosts, is that the quail eat back the foliage, but this is because we are so close to nature. Were our conditions better, I would grow freesias in quantity both for the garden and for cutting, as they are particularly fragrant and attractive for decoration.

TRITONIA CROCATA

Tritonia crocata, sometimes called the flame freesia, is not a freesia, as is obvious from its corm which is like that of a small gladiolus and not like the narrow white bulb of the freesia. It comes only in orange or tomato red, salmon rose, and pink.

Years ago I picked up a lot of the typical orange-red form in an old garden where the bulbs had grown into a great mass. Tritonia crocata seems to be indestructible here, hardier than freesias and thriving under very adverse conditions of heavy soil and even considerable shade. It always attracts attention, but I try to grow it where its striking color will not conflict with others as it is very assertive. In their equal acquiescence in casual conditions the related babianas or baboon flowers are comparable. Their little gladioluslike spikes surmount fuzzier foliage and carry lavender, blue, purple, and crimson flowers, colors which again blend well in mixture. I have always wanted to try Babiana rubrocyanea, which has blue flowers with a red center, but the job of weeding so many little things deters me.

SPARAXIS

Of the minor South Africans I believe the ease of growth, permanence, and colors of the sparaxis particularly commend them to me. They are generally offered only in mixtures, but I have an old red one with a black center, a good white with a yellow center, and I have seen a very fine pure yellow. Sparaxis are invariably healthy here; their small gladioluslike spikes of flowers reappear yearly; and they do not require sunshine to keep them open. A couple of years ago a correspondent in Australia sent me seed of a new strain raised there. I sowed it late in autumn, and this spring, eighteen months later, got flowers. The brilliant colors of the Australian strain and the larger size of the flowers attracted everyone's attention. From the central eyes and the preponderance of red I am sure these great advances are due to the crossing of sparaxis with Streptanthera cuprea, a close relative of vivid orange with a violet

eye, and well worth growing for itself. The Bloem Erf hybrids
—from South Africa but listed in California—are from this
same cross.

IXIAS

Ixias were the first of the South Africans I saw, and I still
believe that in quantity they can give fine garden effects. Ixias
have tall wiry stems studded with many flowers and held well
above the foliage. I cannot say that I care for them in mixtures
as the range of colors, from creamy white through cold pinks,
carmine, yellow, and orange red, often with deeper contrasting centers or eyes, is a bit restless and conflicting, but in separate colors and in closely planted patches the tall stems, waving
in the wind, give pleasant life and color to the spring garden.
The culture of ixias is the same as for other South Africans, but
as their flowers require sunshine to open they are valuable only
for gardens where they can get sun in their season. In our present Berkeley garden, late April and early May fogs have discouraged me from growing them. Even at Stanford the sun was
hardly strong enough to open Ixia viridiflora, which always interests gardeners for its extraordinary coloring—a light green
with a purple eye. Under favorable conditions, ixias self-sow
in California gardens and seedlings spring up near the original
planting, not a wholly unmixed blessing as the resultant colors
are not always good.

GLADIOLUS

While it is true that in certain warm areas along the southern
California coast some varieties of the large summer gladiolus
are planted outdoors for winter or spring cut flowers, this is not
feasible here. When in this chapter I include gladiolus for fall

planting I refer to certain dwarfer and smaller members of the family, of different parentage, which, desirable both for garden and cut flowers, are best planted outdoors in autumn for the dainty spikes they give in April or May. These are now offered mostly in mixtures, but Peach Blossom, low but lovely, the taller salmon-red Spitfire, and the old standard white, The Bride, are now listed. Years ago I imported a fine rose one called Charm which flowered very early; it will eventually get into commerce again through stock I gave to a commercial grower. Well worth considering also is Gladiolus tristis, in the form listed in California, a tall slender thing with graceful straw-colored flowers and a fragrance unique among gladiolus; it is just as easy to grow as the others. All these gladiolus can be left unmoved for several years until their crowding corms require separation and replanting.

NATIVE CALIFORNIANS

This chapter should not be concluded without at least brief mention of our native California spring-flowering bulbs. Here, as in other places having one cold wet season and one warm dry one, nature conserves and perpetuates many of its flowers by providing them with bulbs which grow well below the surface of the soil and carry plants over the long rainless period from June to October. These bulbous plants are less evident than our native annuals and have to be searched for on less traveled back roads or on trails over hills and mountains or along streams, more often appearing in northern than in southern California. In general these natives flower late in spring and close the season on soft notes of wild woodland charm rather than with the heavy brasses of man-made garden flowers like the tulips. As they can only be moved at rest—and at that time cannot be found in their natural haunts, and in any case should not be collected—resort for them must be made to specialists, of whom the late Carl Purdy of Ukiah and, following him, his son, are by far the best known. In fact it is to Mr. Purdy's lifetime of devotion to their popularization that even the all too little garden growing of these native plants is due.

Because in the main their period of flowering conflicts with the iris season—a time when we are not anxious for competing or distracting plantings of other specialties—we have not grown them much of late. Not that they are difficult, for Brodiaea capitata somehow got into the garden and with cultivation has so self-sown that it is almost in the way, though its heads of violet-blue flowers are always pleasing. A few years ago we dug a piece of land and scattered seed of Brodiaea laxa, and for many seasons we have had an annual display of its larger looser umbels of fine blue flowers. I would also have liked plantings of the yellow B. crocea and the scarlet green-tipped B. coccinea which botanists now call Brevoortia Ida-Maia; dealers however stick to the old name. Some brodiaeas seem to do well on our open hillside and in heavy soil, but I believe more kinds thrive in rough, gritty well-drained soils and in partial shade.

Fritillarias are found in the old world as well as the new. One of these, Fritillaria imperialis, the crown imperial, is a striking species, with which I have had no success here, but our native F. lanceolata comes up wild; it is here sometimes called mission bells because of its dark purple bell-like flowers, which are mottled green and make a somber combination. A far finer native species is F. recurva with orange scarlet flowers. The native fritillarias all like well-drained woodsy soils and shade. So do the California erythroniums, the dogs-tooth violets or trout lilies, which my friends who grow them tell me are very easy in loose light moist soil in shade, where they can remain for years and self-sow. I regret I have had no personal experience with them.

CALOCHORTUS AND CAMASSIA

In my early years of California gardening I naturally tried growing calochortus, to me the most exciting of our native bulbs. The lovely little globe tulip, Calochortus albus, and the star tulip, C. maweanus, are woodland plants for the same conditions as the fritillarias but they want less shade; a cool rock garden would provide pockets for them. However, having a preference for the spectacular, I preferred the mariposa or butterfly tulips, particularly forms of C. venustus, with their larger upright cup-shaped flowers on taller stems. These come in yellow, white, and cream, with shadings from pink to purple; many with beautiful base patterns are so desirable that it is worth trying a few in a place which is dry all summer. They are not particular as to soil, coming from rather heavy clayish ones, and some persisted with us for years, but we were discouraged because the gophers here have a liking for the deep-planted little bulbs; if I grew them much I would surround the bed with an underground fence of chicken wire eighteen inches deep. In spite of their popular name, calochortus are of course not real tulips. For the camassias, tall native bulbous plants from places boglike in spring but dry in summer, I have less enthusiasm. At one time we grew Camassia quamash (C. esculenta), used as food by our native Indians, and C. Leichtlinii, with spikes of white or blue star-shaped flowers, but they were unexciting and I did not continue with them. I do not wish to deter others, for the fun of gardening is trying out things oneself.

CHAPTER TWELVE

SUMMER-FLOWERING BULBS AND TUBERS

𝒯HE selection of plants to be discussed in this chapter is somewhat arbitrary, for under California conditions one might often class alstroemerias, cannas, or dahlias as hardy herbaceous plants, and in southern California, in particularly warm areas, the gladiolus can become almost a spring-flowering bulb. Taken as a group, however, the plants included are characterized by bulbous or tuberous roots, and even in California they prefer annual lifting, cleaning, dividing, and replanting. Among them they keep our summer gardens gay and colorful, and if they lack the charm of spring bulbs, they have substantial qualities of size and color plus variety of form and considerable usefulness for cutting; nearly all are of easy culture.

AGAPANTHUS

Agapanthus, the blue lily of the Nile, is a tuberous-rooted evergreen plant from Africa with large umbels of blue, rarely white, flowers. In cold climates it is grown as a tub plant. It is easy—practically indestructible here—and invariably grown in the open ground as a hardy perennial, to be divided only when more plants are wanted or clumps become matted, which is not soon. Though I would prefer to do this from November to April, I would not hesitate to make new plantings at any time.

In the garden I like agapanthus in association with kniphofias and depend each summer on the simple blue and red combination we get from a good blue agapanthus and Kniphofia H. F. Dreer. Frank McCoy, of the Santa Maria Inn, has developed from seed some varieties with larger flowers and in several shades of blue.

ALSTROEMERIA OR PERUVIAN LILY

Alstroemerias, often called Peruvian lilies—though they are not lilies and most of them hail from Chile—are coming into greater use in California as they are nearly all hardy here, grow readily, and are effective both in masses in the garden and for indoor decoration. They must be cut, however, in full flower, never in bud. The only one commonly found is Alstroemeria aurantiaca, which spreads in old gardens by traveling tuberous roots and by self-sown seed, and sends up on tall stiff stems umbels of orange or yellow flowers with darker markings. Far more attractive are the forms of A. chilensis, in a wide range of pastel colors comparable to those of the deciduous azaleas— white, buff, pink, and red, with darker throat markings. These have much grayer foliage than A. aurantiaca. Recently there have been introduced somewhat similar forms of A. Ligtu which grow taller, up to three or four feet, are very vigorous and have larger flowers. These come in a greater variety of the same lovely colors and are long lasting in the garden and really wonderful to cut. The tubers are not commonly offered for sale and are brittle and none too easy to establish. Plant them very deep, eight to ten inches, in autumn or winter, preferably in a light sandy loam. It is really better to raise them from fall-sown seed, scattered either in the open ground—they self-sow very readily when the soil is light and loose—or in flats from which the little plants should be moved into their permanent places while young. Alstroemerias grow well in sun or partial shade, dislike heavy moisture-retentive soils but are otherwise easily satisfied and need no water after their early summer flowering. Their large light umbels topping tall stiff stems give very effective garden color, particularly when they are planted by themselves.

AMARYLLIS

Amaryllis Belladonna (Callicore rosea) sends up bare brown stalks and produces great umbels of pink flowers even in old gardens which have been neglected for years. Because these "naked ladies" are generally poorly planted along walks rather than behind shrubs or plants, which would conceal their lack of basal foliage when they are in flower, amaryllis have been unfairly despised in California. The large bulbs should be planted or replanted in summer—after they lose their leaves and before flower stalks appear—not deep, but with just a covering of soil. They want sun but will put up with partial shade, and they enjoy water even when dormant. Other amaryllis or hippeastrums are in the main grown as pot plants, and their culture cannot be given here.

CANNAS

Cannas can be handled in most of California as hardy herbaceous plants. Busy gardeners often leave them alone from year to year and yet continue to get flowers, but in better culture they are lifted in winter and divided and replanted in early spring. They love rich soil, water, and warm weather, and if you have these conditions, you can use cannas in many ways, formally in beds, as backgrounds in herbaceous borders, even in pots, the softer colors, pinks particularly, combining nicely, though the reds, oranges, and yellows have their places too. If you live in a cool foggy place like San Francisco, forget cannas as they require sun and heat aplenty.

DAHLIAS

Dahlias, on the other hand, revel in coastal conditions, in moisture-laden air and sandy soil, provided this is enriched by cow manure or other fertilizers which may be incorporated in the soil and likewise used for surface feeding when the plants are in flower. Dahlias also like water all through the growing season and are poor, if persisting, without it. The cult of the huge decorative dahlia has always been great in the cooler sections of California, though perhaps these larger dahlias are not as popular as they once were. These are best grown in rows, planted about a yard apart, the single tubers or green plants put in from April through June—if a succession is desired—and each one provided at planting with a strong stake to which it can be attached as heavy growth develops. Show flowers result from fine culture, feeding, and disbudding to a single flower on a stem. Modern taste, especially for garden decoration, is turning to the smaller decorative varieties, which are allowed a freer, more natural growth and the development of quantity rather than specimen bloom; the scale of these smaller kinds is better and they blend well into other plantings, are bright and gay, and give cut flowers more suited to the average room; they are also easier to grow and demand much less attention to thinning and disbudding. The newer dwarf singles—perfectly suited to bedding and giving the maximum for the money— should be more grown in little gardens, particularly as this type, sometimes called Unwin singles, is as easily raised from seed as any half-hardy annual. It can be started in flats and planted out when a few inches high. Of course all dahlias can be raised from seed, and if sown early, they will flower by fall in California, but amateurs will find it better to buy tubers of fine selected and named varieties. After flowering is finished in autumn, even as late as Christmas, the clumps of tubers can be lifted and stored in cool dry places until you are ready in spring to cut them carefully to single tubers—each with a growing eye —for replanting. With many of the more vigorous varieties it is quite possible in warmer sections of the state to leave the tubers in the ground and let them come up again in spring in great clumps. This idea is abhorrent to devotees, but in this way dahlias will still give fair flowers with little effort until they become crowded and have to be lifted and separated.

GLADIOLUS

The gladiolus likewise is a flower which has been for years under process of breeding and improvement, and has many devotees. Its importance as a cut flower transcends its contribution to garden effect, so that it is naturally much grown by itself in rows, in the cutting garden, where by intensive cultivation the finest spikes may be obtained. For this purpose in the warmer parts of southern California it is often planted from late fall in successive lots until the following summer, but throughout northern California planting does not begin until March, when the ground is warming up. Gladiolus are readily grown in any good soil where they may be planted three or four inches deep and six or eight inches apart. Fertilizer should be dug into the ground below the corms so that it will not touch them. Bone meal or any good general commercial fertilizer may be used. Watering must be kept up regularly throughout the growing period, particularly before blooming. Spikes should be cut when the first flowers are fully open and at least five leaves should be left on the plant to enable it to mature next year's corm. New varieties are raised from seed by specialists. Named ones are increased commercially in spring by sowing the bulblets adhering to the old corms. These as a rule must be carried through a second season before they will give even small spikes of bloom.

Before the stalks are quite brown, the corms should be dug and the stems cut off and burned to control thrip, the pest which is now the greatest drawback to gladiolus growing. To control thrip, one prominent California specialist advises storing corms in large paper bags, closed by clips, after placing in each large bag a small open bag containing naphthalene flakes. Before planting, the corms should be peeled and dipped for about two minutes in water, heated to about 120 degrees. Early plantings will often flower before thrips are numerous enough to cause great damage, but a weekly spray made up of one and a half teaspoons of tartar emetic and half a cup of Karo syrup to a gallon of water will ensure their control.

For garden decoration, groups of one variety of gladiolus are most effective, as you will get in that way a fine mass of color rather than a restless effect from many bits of color, some of them clashing. Furthermore, in mixtures the stalks of some varieties will have finished flowering while others are still at their best. For the lazy or overworked gardener there is always the possibility of leaving gladiolus in the ground over winter, a casual method of culture which I have found will give quite fair spikes of bloom rather earlier than those from lifted and replanted corms. I am fortunate in living next to Carl Salbach, in whose growing and breeding gardens I can see superb varieties of gladiolus well grown without any effort on my part.

LILIES

Lilies are among California's more striking natives, but the species all grow at high altitudes or in cool northern coastal country. They want deep planting in autumn, liberal summer moisture, perfect drainage, and a loose friable soil with humus in it. Such are not the common conditions of California gardens and have never been mine, so that I have had only a limited success with lilies. Lilium regale, the regal lily, with pure white, red-throated, sweet-scented flowers, is easy in semi-shade, and good bulbs planted in fall and watered until they flower next June are very rewarding and last here for years. They require no special preparation of the heavy soil in our garden, where they are interplanted with deciduous azaleas. A few bulbs of L. Henryi and L. auratum have managed to persist under the same conditions, but they are not too happy. Years ago we also had large patches of our easiest native, L. pardalinum, the leopard lily, but some virus or other disease carried it off. Unless you have the right conditions or can create them, say in a lath house, I believe it is best to go light on lilies, lovely as they are when well grown.

MONTBRETIAS

Montbretias, which are South African bulbs, can be left in the ground for several years though they are improved by occasional lifting, dividing, and replanting. In old and often neglected gardens they will be seen in summer throwing up branched sprays of red and yellow flowers an inch or so across, bright in the garden, good for cutting, and of the easiest culture. Some years ago a series of wonderfully improved forms, called the Earlham montbretias, came from England, and I grew the largest and most vigorous one, His Majesty, with real satisfaction. If you can now find any of these newer kinds in northern nurseries they are worth a trial as the flowers are three inches across and the spikes large and tall, but they do demand rich soil and far more water than their plebeian ancestors. Apparently their tendency to suffer from thrips and the commercial difficulty of handling a bulb which has only a short season of fall dormancy have mitigated against them as garden plants.

NERINES

Nerines are strangely neglected in California. These fall-flowering South African amaryllids, with umbels of a dozen or more flowers on twelve- to eighteen-inch stems, give colors from white through pink and rose to red, a lovely range, but it is their brilliance, due to a sort of frosted or gold-dusted sheen, which is their greatest attraction. Yet the only good commercial collection I know is that of the Palos Verdes Begonia Farm, which was purchased some years ago from Frank Reinelt, who imported the best named varieties from England and bred many seedlings from them. Those interested in more than I can say here should read his paper, "My Experience with Nerines," in the July, 1946, *Journal of the California Horticultural Society*.

Nerines are not hardy—most of mine were wiped out in the heavy freezes of 1932 and 1937—and they do not like long, cold, early winter rains, so that their outdoor culture in northern California is not very successful. I have found, however, that a vigorous variety of Nerine curvifolia listed as Fothergillii, a glorious glistening red, came through a dozen degrees of frost in my garden, persisted, and still flowers well every autumn in the open ground of a well-drained half shady place. Even in California, except in the most favored places, nerines are best grown in pots and wintered in a cold greenhouse. Use deep pots or redwood boxes—eight inches is a good size—fill them with rich sandy soil and plant the bulbs when dormant in summer, with the upper side just above the soil. The first winter will give you only straplike winter foliage, as nerines resent disturbance, but if watered and fed with a nitrogenous fertilizer, they will reward the grower the next autumn and thereafter for years, undisturbed, crowded in their containers. They like water as soon as the flower stems come through from the leafless bulbs, and when the foliage dies down in summer, they want rest and sunshine. Nerine Bowdenii, somewhat like a small Amaryllis Belladonna, is easier and hardier but lacks the charm of the hybrids.

TIGRIDIAS

Tigridias I had to give up growing as the gophers liked them even more than I did. These tiger flowers, coming in selfs as well as spotted forms, are strange and likable, and their evanescent blossoms certainly interest visitors, but they are purely for garden effect. The general rule is to plant the bulbs, preferably in groups, about three inches deep in spring, and to lift them in late autumn, but from some bulbs the gophers left us, it is evident that in ordinary years our winter cold will allow them to live in the open ground, and so they may remain in place, though this is probably not the preferable way for any but lazy gardeners to treat them.

WATSONIAS

Watsonias from South Africa, with taller stems and smaller flowers than the related gladiolus, are perfectly happy in California, where they should be grown more frequently, especially for their garden value. There are two main groups. Those with deciduous foliage and late spring or early summer flowers are by far the more popular. These, including the many fine hybrids raised in southern California by Mrs. Bullard and in Australia by others, give tall spikes of large open flowers in white, pink, and red of various shades. Plant the bulbs from the end of August through October, early rather than late, as they make immediate fall foliage. No special soil or culture is required, and they may be left undisturbed for some years to form clumps or may be lifted frequently, but in summer, if that is preferred. The species with evergreen foliage, typified by Watsonia Beatricis, never dies down and so is a little harder to move and re-establish. Though I found watsonias tough enough to stand division and replanting in fall, they come so easily from seed that this is a good way to get them. They form big clumps, drought-resistant, easy, colorful in August, but not fine, so they are best relegated to the less tended parts of the garden.

To complete this chapter on a few summer-flowering bulbous plants, I must mention some little things which we have grown with pleasure. Cyclamen neapolitanum, which flowers during the last days of July in considerable shade beneath a copper beech, is a lovely little flower in either the lilac pink or the white form, blooming from its small corms in late summer, when it is leafless, and then throwing up its mottled leaves, which are worth having for themselves. Plant these cyclamens in early summer when they are dormant. Sternbergia lutea, looking like a long-stemmed crocus in October, is such a nice yellow that I grow it, though it is far happier in warmer places, where the bulbs at rest in summer get a long sun baking. Give it a place in the sun, planting the bulbs a couple of inches deep when you can get them, in midsummer, their dormant time. Of the zephyranthes, the best known is the grass-leaved Zephyranthes candida, a bulb of such easy disposition that we have moved it at any time. As long as it gets some summer water it can be depended on for many white flowers and is sometimes used as an edging plant. There are others occasionally offered, of which Z. grandiflora (Z. carinita) is pink, and Ajax, a garden form, is yellow.

CHAPTER THIRTEEN

ANNUALS

CALIFORNIA's greatest contribution to flower gardens has been its annuals. Many of our natives—eschscholtzias, lupines, clarkias, and godetias—have been taken up by plant breeders and greatly improved; others, such as Bartonia aurea (blazing star), Platystemon californicus (cream-cups), and Nemophila insignis (N. Menziesii or baby blue-eyes), have remained in their original character and beauty. Our great spring shows of wildflowers, sheets of blue and gold and pink and yellow, are almost wholly of annuals which, self-sown, spring up with the autumn rains, flower in late winter and spring, and then dry up in the summer drought, leaving their ripened seed to begin the cycle over again.

In gardens these natives and many other annuals, gathered from the ends of the earth and improved for garden purposes, have many uses. In our long growing year some may be sown in the open ground for spring flowering, but even more important is their service in keeping the garden in bloom through the summer months, especially the late ones, when such easy annuals as petunias, verbenas, zinnias, stocks, and marigolds become our mainstays, with shrubs, bulbs, and most perennials then merely a memory. Moreover, annuals furnish continuous supplies of cut flowers, for many of those best adapted to house decoration are of the cut-and-come-again type not often found anywhere but in annuals. Most of them are of easy culture, and coming so readily from seed, offer quantity and variety at a very small cost. Annuals are above all essential in small gardens, because the space they occupy in their time can be used at other times for bulbs or annuals of different season. They are less of an asset in large gardens where labor for their care and replacement may be insufficient.

For purposes of culture or use, no distinction will now be made between true annuals, such as asters and zinnias, and those which flower from seed quite as quickly, like snapdragons or stocks, but under our mild conditions often live into a second year, or even longer. Real perennials, like delphiniums and penstemons, which are often grown in California as annuals, will be found in their proper classification.

TWO METHODS OF SOWING

Of the two methods of sowing annuals—open ground and protected seed beds or flats—the former is best for some, the latter for others, while there are some accommodating ones which can be started in life either way. Broadcasting in fall in the open ground is nature's way. It is from this self-sowing that our wildflowers come, but when conditions for germination or growth are poor in any particular season, we just say that the wildflowers are not good that year. What they want is autumn rain followed by cool weather, and more rain to keep the ground moist over the period of seed germination and early growth. When the early rains are followed by warm weather or drying winds or very cold days, germination and early growth are poor. Furthermore, in nature the annual weeds come up with the annual flowers—California specializes in both—and in seasons of late heavy rains weeds choke out the flowers. In our gardens we can improve on nature.

If the rains come early, let the weeds germinate over the area to be sown later in annuals, then hoe the weeds off in a dry spell. You will thus markedly reduce their competitive or nuisance value. When flower seeds are to be broadcast or sown where they are to flower, prepare the ground by digging and raking in advance and water it so that it is moist, not wet, when seeds are sown. Sow preferably during a cool moist period on a dull, not a bright, day. If the place is small, after the seed has been scattered and raked in give a very light mulch or shade for a few days with branches, lath, even gunny sacking, but this last must be removed before full germination. After that has occurred, watering and especially thinning are necessary; in fact thinning is about the biggest job one has to do with open-ground sowing. Without it success is always limited, as scores of seedlings may come up in the space necessary for one. Even when seed is scattered carefully it is nearly always sown too thickly.

IN THE OPEN

This is the best method for spring-flowering native annuals —poppies, lupines, clarkias, gilias, godetias, nemophilas, phacelias, layias, leptosynes, Platystemon californicus, Collinsia bicolor, and Mentzelia Lindleyi, to mention a selection of those best known. Other annuals, not natives, which are happiest or most effective under this no-transplanting treatment include sweet alyssum, calliopsis, candytuft, Centaurea cyanus, annual chrysanthemums, Dimorphotheca aurantiaca and its hybrids, annual gaillardias, annual larkspurs, linarias, Linum rubrum (scarlet flax), nasturtiums, annual poppies, scabious, schizanthus, Virginian stocks, and viscaria. Some of these will transplant reasonably well, and thinning by that method is possible, but many, the larkspurs, poppies, and sweet peas for example, if transplanted will never really thrive as they do when allowed to flower where they are sown. A few summer-flowering annuals also germinate readily in the open ground and seem to do rather better that way than when transplanted from flats. Cosmos and zinnias come into that class, while some others which are easy to start in the open, but will transplant very well, include calliopsis, Gypsophila elegans, helianthus (sunflowers), marigolds and scabious.

WITH PROTECTION

Success with many annuals is so much more certain if they are given care in their infancy that seed sowing and early culture in prepared seed beds or flats are always recommended. To avoid the perils of open-ground sowing in ordinary soil with beating rains and drying winds or scorching sunshine to contend against, optimum conditions for germination and early life can be provided in specially prepared seed beds with good drainage and fine, friable, light soil mixed with more sand, leaf mold, or peat and rotted manure or rotted vegetation—that is, humus—than our natural soils provide. In California such beds are often best made in lath houses or in frames which can be shaded, initially by muslin, later by laths which can be removed when the plants are able to stand full sunlight. Many gardeners, however, prefer to start their more demanding annuals in flats, giving drainage by holes and a little gravel or broken pot, and filled with similar compost. These flats have the advantage of mobility, and it is easier to sow, water, weed, and later to prick out the seedlings, at table or bench level than on the ground. For the average garden even smaller flat boxes are desirable. If each unit then is kept small, the particular plants in it can be given just what they want without regard to the needs of their neighbors; regimentation is less necessary. Some gardeners now saturate their seed beds or flats with a weed killer two or three weeks before sowing and then sow the seed when its effects have worn off. This saves weeding later, but is less necessary with vigorous annuals than with the slow-germinating seeds of perennials and shrubs.

Seed may be broadcast in flats or sown in very shallow drills across the boxes, the latter method being preferable when seed is scarce or expensive, or when the same flat is being used for small lots of several varieties. Fresh seed of most annuals germinates so freely that thin sowing is desirable, very fine seed having sometimes to be mixed with sand to prevent sowing it too close. Sowing is best done when the soil is just damp, not wet. A very fine spray may be used for watering after sowing and until germination occurs, which with most annuals is within a week. Amateurs should realize that the seed of most annuals retains a very fair, though diminishing, germinating capacity for some years and that, where many plants of some one variety are not wanted in a single season, part of the seed packet may be retained for another year.

After germination and the production of the second, or true, leaves, thinning out is nearly always necessary if the seedlings are to remain in the flats for any length of time. However, far more plants are obtainable and better ones if, after the seedlings have made a couple of weeks' growth, sometimes more, they are pricked out and replanted in seed beds or flats a couple of inches apart, so that they have more room to develop. This is best done by digging up a few seedlings at a time, shaking off the soil, and with a pencil or pointed label or piece of wood, making holes into which they may be dropped. The soil is then pressed firmly around them; they are watered and set in the shade for a few days till established, and then given more sun to inure them to open-ground conditions. Even with sturdy little seedlings it is best to choose cool and foggy days, or at least the late afternoon, for putting them out where they are to flower.

The annuals for which sowing in seed beds or flats is best must naturally be those which transplant readily because they have fibrous rather than tap roots. They include what in catalogs for colder climates are called half hardy annuals, a term of little meaning here, where most of them—not all—could go right through our winters in the open ground. Asters, nemesias, pansies, petunias, pinks, salpiglossis, snapdragons, stocks, verbenas, and zinnias are among the commoner annuals so raised; dwarf single dahlias, penstemons, and other perennials often treated here as annuals also need this careful sowing. Many gardeners prefer to employ it also for many other annuals which, like calliopsis, calendulas, marigolds, or scabious, are adapted either to sowing in open ground or to this segregated and protected treatment. Avoid it for annual larkspurs, eschscholtzias, poppies, sweet peas, or other annuals which resent transplanting.

ANNUALS FOR GENERAL GARDEN USE

The uses of annuals in the garden are many and varied. For color through the late summer and the autumn we are largely dependent on them, on cosmos, marigolds, petunias, and zinnias, to mention only a few. For cut flowers there is a wide range of choice. There are the dwarf things like nemesias, pansies, and calendulas; the taller ones such as the annual larkspurs and lupines; and in summer we can rely on calliopsis and chrysanthemums, cosmos, marigolds, salpiglossis, scabious, and zinnias. Of outstanding value for cutting and available through most of the year are snapdragons and stocks, though stocks for winter flowering will be from quite different hardier strains than the common ten-week varieties grown everywhere for summer beauty. Sweet peas, whose growing is not always easy, will give lovely cut flowers in winter from sowings made in late summer of the winter-flowering strains, and in summer from early spring sowings of the generally finer summer-flowering varieties.

For beds or borders there are many annuals now obtainable from seed in separate colors or in fine mixtures. In southern California and close to the coast farther north, the South African nemesias are wonderfully effective grown by themselves, while in summer, marigolds, petunias, and zinnias are in full flower for months, continuing presentable far into fall. Zinnias, however, are only for warm gardens with lots of sun, water, and feeding. Cosmos can be used for temporary screens or hedges, and cumbent annuals like nasturtiums, the balcony type of petunias, and verbenas are quite satisfactory ground covers for the summer months. Still another purpose to which some annuals can be put is the covering of bulb plantings while the foliage is dying down and after. For this purpose, seeds of calliopsis, annual chrysanthemums, clarkias, godetias, or linarias are sown early among the bulbs, or plants of annuals like petunias, which are reasonably drought-resistant, are set out in early summer between the drying bulb foliage.

232

ANNUALS FOR NATURALIZING

Annuals used for wild gardening, again by themselves, are best sown in autumn with the early rains. These will be predominantly native—lupines, especially the dwarf Lupinus bicolor, nemophilas, phacelias, all blues, eschscholtzias, our native poppy, usually brilliant orange but now obtainable true from seed in more conciliatory yellows, pinks, and reds, and in creamy white. Clarkias and godetias should be in the original forms rather than in the highly developed garden varieties with stronger colors, larger flowers, often doubled, and so suitable only for more formal places. But there are also many annuals, not native sons, which will do well under comparable casual treatment and give the same charming informal effect. Among them are poppies of the single type, particularly the corn poppy and its development, the Shirley poppies, annual larkspurs, candytufts, linarias, Linum grandiflorum (L. rubrum), and the South African dimorphothecas.

ANNUALS IN THE ROCK GARDEN

Being without prejudice as to the inclusion of annuals in rock gardens for pockets or for carpeting, I unhesitatingly recommend to anyone trying to keep a rock garden gay for twelve months a year to call for help on certain dwarf annuals—the little leptosiphons (gilias) with their cream, pink, or golden stars, quite as dainty as any mossy saxifrage; Brachycome iberidifolia, the blue Swan River daisy; Omphalodes linifolia (Cynoglossum linifolium), Venus navelwort, white with gray foliage; Diascia Barberae, pink; Phacelia campanularia, pure blue; Platystemon californicus, cream-cups; Dimorphotheca aurantiaca, orange; Alonsoa Warscewiczii, scarlet; Gypsophila elegans, babys-breath; dwarf sweet alyssum in white or near violet; dwarf candytufts; linarias; nemesias; even the dwarf marigold, Tagetes signata var. pumila (T. tenuifolia). For the heavy names with which many of these delightful little annuals are burdened, I have no responsibility.

ANNUALS IN THE BORDER

I have referred elsewhere to the difficulty of maintaining herbaceous borders without the aid of annuals. Cosmos, the cucumber-leaf sunflowers of graceful branching habit and with markings of red or brown on yellow, even columns of sweet peas of one color, could help out the rear ranks. Marigolds, salpiglossis, scabious, snapdragons, zinnias—all in clumps of one variety, not mixed—would fill in the middle, and edging plants such as I have already suggested for rock gardens could be scattered in groups along the front.

Little space can be given here to a discussion of named varieties of popular annuals or to specific cultures. For many of our gardeners, especially those with small places which they tend themselves all summer, the cult of the annual could be very rewarding, not only in the show it would make, but in the infinite variety available from the more enterprising seedsmen and especially from old English firms like Thompson and Morgan at Ipswich and Suttons at Reading. When I had only a small place to care for, it was my custom every year to search out and plant some new annuals, a hobby appropriate in every way to my resources.

CHAPTER FOURTEEN

ROCK GARDENS, WALL GARDENS, GROUND COVERS

ᴿock gardening apparently had its beginnings in the favorable conditions of the British Isles, and it was there and in the Pacific Northwest that it has had its greatest development. Theoretically it was supposed to be patterned on nature, and infinite trouble was taken to provide highly artificial cultural conditions acceptable to its inhabitants, which were often temperamental alpines. There is really very little reason for us to follow this tradition of rock gardens. Most of our gardens are too small to disguise the fact that they are wholly artificial, most of our gardeners have not the time, or do not choose to give it, for the meticulous culture of plants inherently unhappy here. So let us not regret the passing of what too often resulted from efforts doomed to failure under semiarid conditions. Much too frequently a rock garden becomes just a boulder-strewn area, and when red lava rocks were used, unpardonably ugly. Its justification was that in a small space a lot of plants could be grown; if many of them were difficult, so much the better. This is not enough for most of us; our rock gardens must arise out of natural conditions.

Where there are rough sloping lots, some of the garden can best be handled by rock garden methods, but unless the gardener gets his satisfaction in caring for a plant sanitarium, he had better grow, not the lovelies in English rock garden books but, in the main, tough and fairly drought-resistant plants from climates like ours. Because their bareness when not in flower will never be covered by snow, our rock gardens must be presentable twelve months of the year. This calls for the use of many dwarf evergreen shrubs, of perennials which do not look too shabby in their off seasons, of little bulbs, and of annuals to give bits of color and variety when the big spring show is over.

SUITABLE EVERGREENS

The rock garden is a place to use the many choice little dwarf conifers, horticultural varieties of juniper, spruce, fir, cypress, and others, differing in form, interesting as individuals, slow growing as is desirable, and like some humans always neat and presentable. Also excellent furnishings are provided by the dwarf heathers, forms mainly of Erica carnea and of Calluna vulgaris, evergreen, compact, many very low growing, with flowers of white, lavender, pink, and crimson. These need more water than the big South Africans, but they are worth extra trouble because of their valuable smaller scale and flowers in season. In the rock garden too, the easy Irish heaths, the daboecias, in white, pink, or purple, should be grown. There are also several dwarf or cumbent brooms I grow as rock garden plants, of which Cytisus decumbens is the flattest and C. Ardoinii the dwarfest little upright grower, and my favorite; both have yellow flowers in spring. The hybrids C. Beanii (yellow) and C. kewensis (creamy white) are for rock gardens on a fairly generous scale, as the former makes an eighteen-inch spreading shrub and the latter likes room for its trailing growth, a drop of a foot or two in my garden, where it is less rampant than in the north. The dwarf lavenders and the dwarf rosemary both belong here, and they are fine easy things. There are a number of suitable dwarf cotoneasters, the commonest being the evergreen Cotoneaster microphylla and the deciduous C. horizontalis, but C. Dammeri (C. humifusa) is more prostrate, and C. decora, the necklace cotoneaster, has larger, brighter red berries. For such planting there is also a dwarf form of the evergreen hybrid barberry, Berberis stenophylla var. corallina compacta, with reddish orange flowers.

EMPHASIS ON FLOWERS

The hypericums, with their gay, often cup-shaped, yellow flowers are tempting, but some of them are terribly rampant, have spread too widely, and also self-sow; others, like Hypericum Coris and H. corsicus, are dwarf nonspreading species. Perennial morning-glories sound dangerous, but Convolvulus mauritanicus is a lovely evergreen trailer with lavender flowers. It is a plant which can be easily restrained and is never weedy. Convolvulus Cantabrica and C. cneorum, respectively with pink and white flowers, are little shrubs, not over two feet high, fit nicely into the pockets, and never overrun. The sun roses, helianthemums, are well adapted to rock garden use; there are nice named varieties of reasonably compact growth, like Ben Nevis, and some with more casual, cumbent habit, like Goldilocks, easily the best yellow. Many of what we used to call shrubby veronicas, now named hebes, all from New Zealand, have just the variety of form, like Hebe cupressoides, or the flat habit, like H. chathamica, for rock gardening, but they are only happy in cool situations along the coast. There is one little daphne, which is none too easy here, though it is a great grower farther north. It seems to want an acid soil, light shade, and summer water. My plants grew well enough but fail to flower, and it is for their fragrant little pink heads they are grown. In any case Daphne cneorum is worth trying.

SUCCULENTS

Another way to keep our rock gardens looking well all year is to plant a due proportion of succulents—sedums, sempervivums, the choicer mesembryanthemums, even dwarf aloes. Succulents are often very effective. They provide a most interesting variety of color and form in their foliage as well as in their flowers. Collectors tend to consider the more showy things even if they are tender, but general gardeners will do well to limit the use of succulents outdoors to those of demonstrated ability to take as much winter frost as your garden ever gets.

PERENNIALS

Of small herbaceous perennials, suitable for California rock gardens, there is a great variety of reasonably tough drought-resistant ones to meet most desires, without including such problem children as gentians and other alpines. Our best doers will be apt to come from countries of dry summers and not from the high Alps, Rockies, or Sierras. Some of them have persistent foliage and under our conditions might just as well be classed as subshrubs.

Proceeding alphabetically, I start with the aethionemas, Persian candytufts, dwarf shrublets here, and being Mediterraneans, quite happy. Aethionema grandiflora and Warley Rose are about the best bets. Alyssum saxatile is indestructible and spreads and self-sows here. The typical forms are suited only to planting on a large scale, but there are more compact forms, and the free-growing ones stand restraint and do not spread underground. Arabis albida is somewhat less rampant and enjoys more water and shade, but is also very easy in any soil. There are single white and pink forms, also a double white, which I prefer. Arenaria montana is a slender trailer with white flowers, an easy sun lover. Aster alpinus has not been contented at our altitude. Of course, the dwarf hybrids referred to elsewhere can be used in rock gardening, but they require yearly division and replanting. Aubrietias are invaluable; either in patches, pockets, or trailing over walls these Grecian plants give wonderful spring color in lavender, purple, and pink, and aubrietias are of the best disposition. They come readily from seed, and there are a few named varieties, of which Vindictive, a rich red purple, is one of the best.

Campanulas have many dwarf species and varieties, of which some require cooler, moister conditions than California gardens offer, but Campanula isophylla is an easy late summer-flowering trailer, its foliage almost concealed by dozens of flat white starry flowers; there is also a blue variety, less vigorous with me, which I got as C. isophylla var. Mayi. Campanula Portenschlagiana (C. muralis) also flourishes; indeed it is sometimes used as a ground cover or for edging; its mats of deep green foliage are covered with starry violet flowers in early summer. Campanula Poscharskyana—sorry about these names, for which I repeat I am not responsible—is another Dalmatian species everyone can grow, a trailer with blue flowers. On a dry bank in San Francisco I noticed C. rotundifolia, the harebell, throwing up its flower spikes a foot or more high at the end of July, an easy doer and a species with many varieties. Other campanulas are worth trying in rock gardens, but start with these.

Cerastium tomentosum, a creeper with small gray leaves and white flowers, is almost too easy and has to be restrained, which is easily done. Ceratostigma plumbaginoides (formerly Plumbago Larpentiae) is also easy and drought-resistant, but less rank in growth; dwarf and slow spreading, its merits are in its really blue flowers, borne above bronzy foliage late in summer.

Dianthus gives us a lot of perennial pinks, dwarf enough for rock gardens. Most of the family are happy here, but Dianthus alpinus and D. neglectus are not, and in spite of all our efforts, though they were lovely, they left us. The small easy rock species, D. deltoides, the maiden pink, persists here without special care, and its pink or white flowers are appreciated. For casual gardeners, good dwarf selected forms of D. plumarius or hybrids from it are best. We recently added what is possibly one of them, Little Joe, which has a nice compact habit and large crimson flowers, off and on all summer.

Erigeron mucronatus (often listed as Vittadinia triloba) is a small pink and white trailing daisy which comes up here from self-sown seed in walls and pockets. It is easy, sometimes too prevalent, but so happy one cannot leave it out altogether. Gypsophila repens is a little trailer with pinkish white flowers, easily satisfied, and Iberis sempervirens, an evergreen white candytuft, is the most perennial of that family here.

The dwarf bearded irises, though their season is short and they need occasional transplanting, can be used, as they are tough and drought-resistant. So too is the much daintier Iris innominata, and I prefer its more slender orange flowers at about the same time in spring. Not so easy, but doing well here where it gets regular watering, is I. gracilipes.

Lithospermum prostratum seems to be difficult for some gardeners, but years ago when we put out a small plant of the variety Heavenly Blue in a mixture of light soil and peat with a little lime—as we were advised to do—it slowly took hold, eventually made big mats, and then from self-sown seed in the ordinary heavy soil here, it went to town; it wants summer water. The variety Grace Ward is also doing well and has much larger flowers of the same true blue. Nepeta Mussini is perfectly easy, but a bit big and spreading. Nierembergia rivularis, from Argentina, was reputed difficult to establish, but this creeper with white cups spread so by underground growth we had to give it up altogether.

Phlox subulata, with prickly foliage, a creeper and a hanger, gives us many colors in this easy species, all spring bloomers. Camlaensis, reputed to be a variety, is far superior and easily our favorite, a grand easy rock garden plant, with better foliage and larger, brighter salmon-pink flowers than any P. subulata I have seen. Primulas are mostly moisture loving, but seedlings of P. acaulis (P. vulgaris) come up here in chinks in the rocks. Saponaria ocymoides is very accommodating, a trailer, making a curtain of green covered with pink flowers every spring.

The thymes, some bushy, some creepers, are among our very best rock plants, with white, lavender, pink, or red flowers and a great variety of odors, a family worth cultivating. The creepers are mainly forms of Thymus Serpyllum, while T. vulgaris, T. nitidus, and T. Herba-barona are examples of shrubby thymes. Among the herbaceous veronicas are some that are adapted to rock gardens. Vinca minor, the common periwinkle or running myrtle, is an easy trailer, with blue, white, and double forms; they like shade. The easier violas can also be used, where some shade and moisture can be given.

To supplement all these, small bulbs may be planted in clumps—snowdrops, crocus species, cyclamen, muscari, miniature narcissus, Triteleia uniflora, Sternbergia lutea, and others. Even little annuals can be sown to fill in blanks—linarias, leptosiphons, Virginian stocks, and many others of appropriate size.

RETAINING WALLS

So many California gardens are on hillsides that dry-rock retaining walls often have to be used to hold up terraces, and even the upper edges of paths have to be margined with a single tier of stones to retain the earth. In chinks in higher walls and gaps in lower ones, and always on top, many rock plants can be set where their beauty will be seen readily. A due proportion should be trailers, plants like Campanula isophylla or Cytisus kewensis, which will drape themselves over and down the face of the wall. This use of functional structure, rather than ineffective attempts to imitate nature in rock gardens, seems to have greater justification in our day.

GROUND COVERS

Not unrelated is the problem of covering the ground, often sloping ground, in a state where there is no natural perennial green sod. Lawns are expensive, require much care—cutting, watering, and replacement—but as with some other luxuries, we insist on them. Substitutes like lippia, strawberry, or dichondra are rarely wholly satisfactory. Where they are hardy and the soil is sufficiently sandy, mesembryanthemums offer possibilities; so do a variety of other dwarf succulents, if the area to be covered is not too large. Creeping thymes, gazanias, Convolvulus mauritanicus, and helianthemums are practical on a small scale. Hypericum calycinum is tough, spreading, evergreen, and drought-resistant. Some of the dwarf natives, like Ceanothus gloriosus, are excellent on slight slopes. Cotoneasters, particularly Cotoneaster horizontalis and C. microphylla, are often grown to cover banks; personally I prefer the rarely found C. congesta. Junipers are among the best ground covers, requiring little care, and they are fairly permanent. On banks and slopes, Lantana sellowiana, Lonicera japonica (a nearly evergreen honeysuckle), ivy geraniums, and in shade or cool places ivy itself are all being used. For large areas on steep slopes, mixed shrubberies of drought-resistant things, native ceanothus, brooms, cistus, barberries, and dozens of others have in my own experience been the answer.

CHAPTER FIFTEEN

GARDENS OF MY DREAMS

———————

My DREAMS of gardens are daydreams, never nightmares. During the relative unconsciousness of sleep, my dreams with all their joys, fears, and absurdities seem to have been unconcerned with gardening. I have never awakened from a vision of a garden in which the climate could be controlled by a switch, and sun, rain, and fog turned on and off at will. I have never dreamed of a garden always in perfect bloom when visitors arrived; nor have I ever come out of a nightmare in which the elements or gigantic insects have destroyed the garden. I haven't achieved in a dream a perfect iris or daffodil for which I had worked for years and then awakened to disappointment.

My dreams of gardens have been attempts at fulfillment in my mind of ambitions or plans beyond my time, my resources, or the climate in "that state into which it hath pleased God to call me." They have been conscious efforts to escape from limitations imposed on one feeble individual and are concerned with the gardens I cannot have, though they may be available to others. My dreams in fact have been reveries—exercises in imagination. Sometimes they have led to time-consuming but innocuous blueprints for carrying them out, but they have proved less dangerous forms of escape than the more subjective efforts of some individuals to get around the monotony of a single personality by vain imaginings which may adversely affect other human beings.

When I am in the high mountains, let us say at Lake Tahoe, I like to dream of a garden where the perfect rest of winter, with its deep snow blanket, and a relatively short and never dry summer, would permit the growing of all the things ill adapted to my present garden—alpines, eastern wildflowers, dogwoods, lilacs, and lilies; but it is really as well that I cannot have a subirrigated mountain meadow as I need a vacation from gardening in summer. And often when on various trips I see the beauty and interest of our native flora, I marvel that more gardeners do not specialize in our California natives as does Louis L. Edmunds with shrubs in his Danville garden, or as is done at the Santa Barbara Botanic Garden, and I read over Lester Rowntree's books, and Carl Purdy's and Theodore Payne's catalogs, and dream of the trees and shrubs, the perennials, bulbs, and annuals we have and use so little, and how a wonderful garden could be made from them alone—if one were willing so to restrain himself.

Though I have never been able to achieve them, I still dream of separate walled gardens on level ground, in which one could grow specialties—irises or gladiolus or roses—gardens which could be visited and shown to friends when in full flower and their existence ignored when they were no longer attractive.

THE PERFECT ROSE GARDEN

I dream especially of a rose garden. Though I have grown roses in all three of my California gardens they have never been featured. Sometimes I have had just a big bed, sometimes a border, sometimes roses interplanted with other things. Roses can be so grown, and some of them, the polyanthas, make excellent path plantings. And certainly climbing roses can be used variously on houses, fences, over arches, and to screen garages and sheds. But for their garden effect and for ease and perfection of culture, they call for segregation into separate gardens where their needs can best be met and where they will not be too prominent when their season of bloom is over, for it must be acknowledged that from November to April—when they are at rest or have been pruned back for the next season's flowering —they are not beautiful and interest in them is only in anticipation.

The rose garden I dream of would be on level ground. Otherwise expensive terracing for beds would be necessary and tiresome climbing for those visiting the garden. It would preferably be enclosed, and though this might be done acceptably in the middle of one's larger garden by surrounding the bushes with a hedge, I would prefer my rose garden in a small place at the rear, with a nice wide path, planted to polyanthas, leading to it. The division from the general garden would be a pergola for social purposes and to provide a place for many climbing roses; the other walls would be latticed for the same purpose, if the pergola did not extend all round. The plan would be quite formal, for the modern rose is an artificial product, developed as a flower-producing machine, and it is well to acknowledge this in its surroundings. The beds would tend to be long and narrow, and there would be convenient paths so that at all times the bushes would be accessible for care and culture and the flowers could be seen close at hand. In selecting varieties I would have beds of one or, at most, two kinds which would go well together, all of well-tried varieties which by experience I had found adapted to my conditions—perhaps the most important consideration. In a not too conspicuous place I would have also a large bed for the trial of new varieties, for the interest and excitement of it and for selection of replacements as the older kinds were being superseded. Visiting local trial and show gardens and meeting with other rosarians would help me to know the newer kinds, but I would want my own experiences as well.

The culture of roses has been too demanding for a general gardener like myself to specialize in them, but even in my dream garden I would not go to excess, as have some fanatics, in preparation of the ground. Most California garden soils will grow roses if they are dug to a depth of at least eighteen inches, but they will be greatly improved if twenty-five per cent of the total bulk of soil is made up of peat or other humus well incorporated into it. Old cow manure, free of vicious weeds, cannot be beaten as a fertilizer, but it often cannot be found. Alfalfa meal or any good commercial fertilizer like ammophos, containing a fair percentage of phosphoric acid, will feed roses adequately, and manure mulches and top dressings help greatly. Pruning is something which must be learned and comes with experience and the study of individual varieties. Let it be light rather than heavy, with no long-stemmed cutting; that is the florist's job. Especially is it important to prune sparingly until roses are a year or two old and have made that top growth which many varieties require for adequate flower production.

Insects, thrips especially in some sections, are a great nuisance; the spray of sugar and tartar emetic, mentioned under gladiolus, should be used to kill them off. Other sprays are available for chewing insects. Mildew affects many roses. I would grow preferably those least affected and use dusting sulphur or other specifics to abate mildew when climatic conditions brought it on, as they do from time to time. Watering of roses would be continuous and adequate; they love water, but no rules can be given because garden conditions govern need. With these simple directions perhaps you can achieve this rose garden of my dreams, which my dry hillside garden and preoccupation with many other things may never let me have.

A LATH HOUSE

I have always dreamed of a lath house, not merely the strictly functional structure, which is like an overventilated shed with its walls made of laths set their own width apart and running up and down to a height of seven feet, and with a similar roof of laths running north and south—this arrangement being best for tempered light and sunshine. Rather, I dream of a structure —designed by an architect who would be also a gardener—with proper proportions and some style of its own. Though I realize that something quite simple and primitive will do to give desired shade and, quite as important, to temper the wind, I would like the structure to be attractive as it would house much beauty and contain more plant perfection than can be expected outside of its protective limits. In winter and spring it could be largely forgotten, though ferns would be happy there through the year and so would camellias and azaleas, but I prefer to grow these outdoors in my garden. Polyanthus primroses would then cover the ground in my lath house and show there a vigor and perfection of flower and color rarely possible outdoors. I might even try a few of the candelabra primroses from China. Some of the late daffodils too would be better for lath protection.

But it would be in summer that this lath house would come into its own, when it would chiefly house lilies, fuchsias, and begonias, particularly the tuberous ones. Garden conditions in California are not commonly favorable to lilies, but the artificial ones possible in a lath house—semishade without interference from hungry tree roots and moisture in the ground and the air— would make easy here the growing of many lilies for which we envy the gardeners of cooler climes. Fuchsias could be espaliered around the walls and grown as standards in tubs, and perhaps a few of those of very drooping habit could be grown in pots or redwood boxes hanging from the roof. Under such conditions they could be treated like aristocrats, well cared for, with the food, water, and shade they love. But chiefly would I grow tuberous begonias there with a perfection I never found possible when years ago I sought shady places in our garden and used the begonias as bedding plants. True, they made a certain show, but after every trip to Capitola to see how Frank Reinelt grew them, I came to the conclusion that here was a plant which demanded special consideration and should be given it; it will stand no rivals in its time.

TUBEROUS BEGONIAS

Tuberous begonias are not really difficult plants. Like some human beings they just say, "Give us everything we want and we will be perfectly happy." Their culture is not complicated. The common way to grow them is to buy tubers sometime between January and March; these were developed the previous year by commercial growers who raised the plants from seed, flowered them, and harvested the one-year tubers after the foliage died down in late autumn. If placed in open trays, just slightly moistened, they will soon show growing points. Fill flats then with a mixture of sand and leaf mold or sand and peat, place the tubers three or four inches apart with the tops about half an inch below the surface, keep them moist but not wet, and grow them on until the sprouts are three or four inches high. Then transplant into pots, redwood boxes, or open ground. As the beauty of begonias is in the individual flower, I prefer them in pots or boxes on benches, or hanging in the case of the basket or pendent varieties. The preference of the tuberous begonias is for light sandy soils, composed largely of humus, leaf mold, or peat. They are good feeders, and for the finest flowers Frank Reinelt—whose recommendations I would follow—suggests mixing either fish meal or cottonseed meal with the soil in the lower half of the container so that the plants will reach it as they grow. He would supplement this by a tablespoon of additional fertilizer later in the season, this being kept away from leaves or tuber by making a shallow furrow around the edge of the pot, putting it in this, and then covering with soil. Watering is very important, just a gentle spray until the plants get going, then regular supplies but never from hard packing streams. For the finest effects he reduces the growths to a single stem; this does not refer to hanging varieties. In autumn as the foliage turns yellow, water is diminished until the plants die down, then all soil is gently washed off and the tubers stored in a cool dry place over winter. They increase in size and can be used from year to year, producing larger plants as they themselves grow in size and require larger pots.

In California, where most tuberous begonias are raised commercially, it is possible, between May 15 and June 15, to buy young seedling plants, large enough then to ship well within the state; these will be cheaper than tubers, and if grown on as recommended, they will flower during the cooler days of autumn, continuing the show and providing an opportunity for gardeners in warmer sections to grow tuberous begonias after their hot summer is over. Raising them from seed requires special facilities.

The culture of hanging begonias is much the same as for others in pots, but here, as mass effects are wanted, larger tubers are desirable; by pinching the top growths to induce branching a wider spread may be obtained. Glazed pots rather than porous ones, or redwood boxes, not wire baskets, are recommended.

I have watched yearly the constant improvement in habit, size, and variety of form, and in the widening range of luscious colors, with new pastel shades and picotee patterns of entrancing loveliness, and so I dream of growing tuberous begonias some day.

AUTUMN COLOR

I do not dream of the eastern American spring—for to appreciate the wonder of its awakening one has to get thoroughly tired of winter—but for its lovely coloring, I do envy easterners their autumn as the days grow shorter and colder and there is a tang in the air and the smell of smoke and of rain. I still miss the brilliance of fall foliage and have made spasmodic efforts to suggest it in my garden, and I dream of a garden which could be developed around the idea of autumn color—yellows, reds, bronzes, and browns. At that time the lavender of the tree dahlia or other pallid colors seem to me out of season. Cosmos, I feel, come in the wrong colors for fall, so do petunias and stocks.

In such a garden for autumn few annuals could be featured. Marigolds would be about the best and the bronzes, browns, yellows, and reds of the big zinnias. Snapdragons would fit, but are not easy to have at their best then. Among perennials there are not many for California gardens as the usual late things of colder climates—helianthus, heleniums, rudbeckias, all the red and yellow daisy tribe—are over here long before October and November. But we do have chrysanthemums and, if emphasis is placed on midseason and late pompons, singles, and smaller decoratives, they alone will give lots of the color range desired, while the early varieties and all the pink and rose-colored ones are omitted. Among succulent plants there are some good late-flowering things in the right color range, the aloes for example.

It is, however, on deciduous shrubs and trees we must chiefly depend, and we do not have many of these with fall foliage turning red and yellow in a climate where there is no autumn frost. Berries are more apt to furnish reds and yellows, and among the cotoneasters and pyracanthas, discussed elsewhere, will be found mention of those which have proved most effective. My experience has been that birds do not go after pyracantha berries, which in any case are far more numerous and more colorful than those of any other berry-bearing shrub. Since their greatly increased planting in Berkeley gardens in recent years, there is really a lot of fall color here, and it lasts well into the New Year.

The fruits of certain small trees will help in this project. The mountain ash, Sorbus Aucuparia, sets berries early and gives good color well above the ground, and the pinnate foliage is very pleasant. The haws or fruits of certain American hawthorns—little seen here—can be obtained by planting Crataegus Crus-galli, the cockspur thorn, which has as beautiful berries as any I know, but if only one hawthorn is planted, I would give preference to Crataegus cordata (now called C. Phaenopyrum), the Washington thorn of Virginia and from the Atlantic coast south. This has the further merit here of having foliage which turns lovely shades of red and metallic bronze in autumn.

The crab-apples are a bit early in coloring and maturing their fruit, many of them, notably the red Siberian crab, being at their best and ready for jelly making in August and September, but Pyrus Eleyii and P. aldenhamensis are much later, and their large cherry red fruits persist here into October.

We simply cannot compete with colder climates in fall foliage, but there are a number of deciduous shrubs which color nicely; the mollis azaleas are getting red by late August, but it will be October before the viburnums turn; V. opulus and V. tomentosum have the asset of rich autumn color as well as their lovely flowers in spring. The trees most recommended for fall color in California are the sweet gum, Liquidambar styraciflua, red and persistent; the scarlet oak, Quercus coccinea, slow growing here but lovely when it gets large enough to have a lot of deep lustrous red leaves in autumn—there are several street plantings of it in Berkeley—and the Chinese pistache, Pistacia chinensis, with bright red pinnate leaves. For yellow autumn foliage we can use Gingko biloba, the maidenhair-tree, a fine specimen tree at any time. Away from the cool coast, at Stanford, for example, but not at Berkeley, the tall Lombardy poplars turn in autumn to pillars of pale gold. That I have not mentioned certain natives—Cornus Nuttallii, the western dogwood, of unexcelled red autumn color in the high mountains; the aspens, equally striking in gold at high altitudes; or Cercis occidentalis, the western redbud, wine red when summers are hot—is because these are either too difficult to grow here or would not color up under our conditions. I have also omitted trees like the Japanese maples, the purple beech, and the purple-leaved plums because their coloring is not of autumn alone and has no nostalgic charm for me.

Everyone who has driven through Bartlett pear orchards must have noticed the warmth of color the leaves develop in autumn, metallic shades of red and bronze, but our couple of trees in the fog belt fail to develop any fall color. Our main dependence, and it has never failed us, is on the flowering Japanese cherries, all of which give us our best autumn leaf color, though the taller, stronger growing singles like Prunus yedoensis and Mikuruma Gaeshi (Mitchell's single pink) are far more striking than the rather dumpy doubles, and in fall they give us as lovely leaf color against the blue autumn sky as their white and pink blossoms do in spring. They would be—as they are here—featured trees in my dream garden of autumn color.

Like a man dying of thirst in the desert, my last dream is of water, not for myself but for my garden. It is a dream of a garden so well supplied with cunningly contrived sprinklers that by a twist of the wrist the particular place needing gentle rain would get it even in our driest months, and incidentally the controls would always be of easy access and far enough from the spray so that I also would not get wet. A wise friend of mine, a native son and a fine gardener, says that in California no man is lazy enough to water his garden by hose or by hand; we must give our gardens more than that and in gentle artificial rains. With this sage advice—which it has taken me nearly a lifetime to learn—I send forth this book in the hope my experience may help other amateur gardeners in their adventurous and happy hobby.

INDEX

Index